Are You Ready for a Capital Campaign?

Assessing Your Nonprofit's Ability to Run a Major Fundraising Campaign

Linda Lysakowski, ACFRE

*Charity*Channel®
PRESS™

Are You Ready for a Capital Campaign? Assessing Your Nonprofit's Ability to Run a Major Fundraising Campaign

One of the **In the Trenches**™ series
Published by
CharityChannel Press, an imprint of CharityChannel LLC
30021 Tomas, Suite 300
Rancho Santa Margarita, CA 92688-2128 USA
http://charitychannel.com

ISBN: 978-1-938077-12-8

Library of Congress Control Number: 2013934998

13 12 11 10 9 8 7 6 5 4 3 2

Printed in the United States of America

This and most CharityChannel Press books are available at special quantity discounts for bulk purchases for sales promotions, premiums, fundraising, or educational use. For information, contact CharityChannel Press, 30021 Tomas, Suite 300, Rancho Santa Margarita, CA 92688-2128 USA. +1 949-589-5938

Foreword

I t is so tempting and so easy to think that a capital campaign will solve your organization's financial challenges. Logic would be on your side. Recurring needs are not being met year after year, and the perfect solution would be to engage the entire organization, its board, staff, supporters, and the community to embrace the "new direction and concentration of energy" toward a comprehensive capital campaign.

Sometimes this is the winning solution, and all involved are happy because they can feel the satisfaction of knowing the organization is on a more solid foundation than if it merely increased its annual fundraising goals. However, many organizations struggle and belabor the issue of whether they should do a capital campaign. I would add to this quandary list whether they should do any campaign, including an endowment campaign.

So now we have the perfect litmus test for these important questions—Linda's workbook. Linda takes us on the journey of exploring the differences of an annual campaign versus a capital campaign, the resources needed of human capital and financial capital, governance issues, and a great surprise ending—what do you do if you determine your organization is not campaign-ready?

We all prepare for meetings, prepare for our events, prepare our boards, and prepare our asks. Now it is time to spend our energy and prepare our organizations to examine the "campaign readiness" test, and Linda's workbook is our guide to finding our answer.

Laura Fredricks, Author
The ASK—How to ASK for Your Nonprofit Cause, Creative Project and Business Venture (Jossey-Bass 2010) and *Winning Words for Raising Money* (Jossey-Bass 2013)

Acknowledgments

I would like to thank all of my colleagues in capital campaigning, including the clients and consultants I've worked with over the years. Many of the questions discussed in this book are from the Campaign Readiness Tool developed by and used with the permission of Marc Lee, CFRE; John Fettig; and Paul Strawhecker, ACFRE. I especially want to thank these colleagues for their valuable contributions to the fundraising profession.

About the Author

Linda Lysakowski, ACFRE, is one of approximately one hundred professionals worldwide to hold the Advanced Certified Fund Raising Executive designation. In her twenty years as a philanthropic consultant, Linda has managed capital campaigns ranging from $250,000 to more than $30 million, helped hundreds of nonprofit organizations achieve their development goals, and trained more than 25,000 professionals in Canada, Mexico, Egypt, Bermuda, and most of the fifty United States in all aspects of philanthropic development.

Linda has received the Outstanding Fundraising Executive award from both the Eastern Pennsylvania and the Las Vegas chapters of AFP (Association of Fundraising Professionals). In 2006, Linda was recognized internationally with the Barbara Marion Award for Outstanding Service to AFP.

Linda is a graduate of Alvernia University with degrees in banking & finance and theology/ philosophy and a minor in communications. As a graduate of AFP's Faculty Training Academy, she is certified as a Master Teacher. She is a member of the board of directors of the AFP Foundation and past president of the AFP Sierra Chapter in Reno, Nevada. She is a frequent presenter at regional and international conferences and has received two AFP research grants.

Linda is the author of *Recruiting and Training Fundraising Volunteers*; *The Development Plan*; *Fundraising as a Career: What, Are You Crazy?*; *Capital Campaigns: Everything You NEED to Know*; *Raise More Money from Your Business Community*; *Fundraising for the GENIUS*; a contributing author to *The Fundraising Feasibility Study—It's Not About the Money*; co-editor of *YOU and Your Nonprofit*; and co-author of *The Essential Nonprofit Fundraising Handbook*. Contact Linda at www.lindalysakowski.com.

Introduction

While there is no strict formula for determining whether any capital campaign will be successful, certain key indicators will help you determine whether your campaign will succeed. These indicators include the board's readiness to support the campaign, an organizational infrastructure to manage the campaign, and the community's willingness to get involved in the project. As I wrote my book, *Capital Campaigns: Everything You NEED to Know,* I tried to keep these principles in mind and provide a guide that would cover the basics of successful campaigns.

I received many comments from people about the book. I found that there was a recurring theme: many people wanted checklists that would help them better prepare for their campaigns. Hence, this workbook was developed to help you lead your staff, board members, and volunteers through the process of preparing effectively for your capital campaign. I encourage you to use the workbook to accompany your readings on capital campaigns.

On the pages that follow, you will find questionnaires, checklists, and other tools to help you assess your readiness for a capital campaign. In addition, I have included sidebars that will draw attention to some of the key indicators of success, definitions of terms that might be unfamiliar to novice fundraisers, and tips to help you succeed with your campaign.

Before we start, let's review exactly what a capital campaign is and what makes it different from your annual fundraising efforts.

While the difference between an annual campaign and a capital campaign might seem like basic common sense (i.e., that the goal is larger, and the money raised is used for major capital expenditures, rather than operating budget), one important thing to note is that your donors will think differently about a capital campaign. They will be making significant contributions—perhaps the largest gift they've ever made—so these contributions will generally come from accumulated assets and/or will be paid over time. In other words, capital campaign gifts are not usually a "write out a check" gift. Donors will think of their capital campaign gifts as "investments" in your organization, the way they might think of investing in a home or their children's education, and not as ongoing expenses like buying groceries or filling their gas tanks. The good news for you is that you can still ask your donors for annual gifts, even while conducting a major capital campaign.

The chart shows differences between an annual giving and a capital campaign.

Annual Giving	Capital Campaign
Ongoing, every year	Defined, limited period of time
Supports operating budget	Supports capital expenses: new construction, renovation, major repairs, major equipment, and/or endowment
Staff-driven	Volunteer-driven
Smaller, individual goals	Large, combined goal
Current-year payments	Multi-year pledges
Heavy direct-response solicitations	Heavy personal solicitation
Gifts from "disposable income"	Gifts from "accumulated assets"

One of the most exciting parts of a capital campaign, to me, is that an organization is so different after a capital campaign than it was going into it. The intensity of a campaign, the number of volunteers involved, the increased public awareness, and the improved infrastructure will make your organization stronger than ever. So fear not: Forget the "pain" and focus on the positive side of your capital campaign.

Chapter Summary

Chapter One: Planning for a Capital Campaign

As with any fundraising activity, it is important to have a plan in place. The ready, fire, aim approach does not work with any fundraising, but is especially dangerous in a capital campaign. Why? The capital campaign is generally the most publicly visible fundraising activity your organization will ever attempt. You *must* get it right. In this chapter I will walk you through exercises to help you plan for success.

Chapter Two: Donor and Community Relations

It might sound obvious, but you can't run a successful campaign without donors. Do you have donors who support your organization faithfully? Do you have donors who could and would supply leadership-level gifts to your campaign? I will provide checklists in this chapter to help you assess your current donor relations and your potential for involving major donors in your campaign.

Chapter Three: Financial Considerations

The long-held premise that it takes money to make money has perhaps never been truer than in capital campaigning. During a campaign, it is critical that you can show donors that your organization is viable, that you have a strong financial position, and that you can deliver on what you promise. You will need to budget for campaign expenses. I will provide, in this chapter, tools to help strengthen your financial position.

Chapter Four: Mission, Vision, and Planning

All campaigns should begin with the strategic planning process. We know that people give to people, not to buildings or endowments, so your plan should demonstrate how this project will help the people you serve. In this chapter, I will guide you through the strategic planning process.

Chapter Five: The Planning Study

In almost every case, it is wise to conduct a planning (or feasibility) study before you launch a capital campaign. An independent assessment of your organization's readiness to conduct a campaign, as well as the community's likelihood to support a campaign, will help you start on the right foot. I will provide you with some basics about the study, discuss who should conduct your study, and describe how the results can help you prepare for a successful campaign.

Chapter Six: Executive Leadership Experience

Your executive director, president, or chief administrator will need to devote a great deal of time to the campaign. This chapter will help you assess your CEO's willingness and ability to devote sufficient time to identify, cultivate, and solicit leadership gifts for the campaign. I will provide you with the tools to assess the strengths of your CEO and how these strengths can facilitate a successful campaign.

Chapter Seven: Development Staff

Every organization that plans a capital campaign needs to assign someone to manage the campaign internally. Whether you have a small, large, or nearly nonexistent development staff, the campaign will require both time and expertise from the entire development team, including board and executive staff members. This chapter will assist you in assessing your staff strengths and weaknesses. I will provide ideas to help your current staff prepare, and/or discuss hiring staff, to manage the campaign.

Chapter Eight: Donor Records and Development Office Infrastructure

Attempting to run a capital campaign without the proper infrastructure in place is like trying to cross the country without roads, bridges, or power. You must have certain components in place internally before you can consider a capital campaign. In this chapter, I will provide you with tools to help assess your organization's infrastructure. I will also offer tips on what you can do to build the basic groundwork for a successful campaign.

Chapter Nine: Governance

Your board members will be the champions of your campaign. Without the support of your board, it will be impossible for the campaign to succeed. The exercises in this chapter will help you evaluate the size, strength, and diversity of your board, as well as its willingness to support the campaign financially, emotionally, and physically.

Chapter Ten: Volunteer Roles and Responsibilities

Often during a capital campaign, hundreds of volunteers are involved. From the top-level volunteers, the campaign chair(s), to phone and mail volunteers, the role of volunteers lends credibility to your campaign, builds enthusiasm, and helps staff accomplish all of the necessary tasks. In this chapter I will provide tools to assess the types and number of volunteers your campaign will need and determine how to find good volunteers.

Chapter Eleven: Developing a Plan to Proceed (or Not) with Your Campaign

If you are ready for a capital campaign, what are the first steps? If you are *not* prepared for a campaign, what do you do to get there? This chapter answers those questions and more. I will provide checklists that will help prepare your organization for a successful campaign or, if you aren't quite ready yet, to regroup and remodel your organization for a future campaign.

Publisher's Acknowledgements

This **In the Trenches**™ workbook was produced by a team dedicated to excellence; please send in your feedback to editors@charitychannel.com.

We first wish to acknowledge the tens of thousands of nonprofit-sector peers who call charitychannel.com their online professional home. Your enthusiastic support for the **In the Trenches** series is the wind in our sails.

Members of the team who produced this book include:

Editors

Acquisitions Editor: Amy M. Eisenstein

Comprehensive Editor: MaryBeth Harnisch

Copy Editor: Jo Alice Darden

Production

In the Trenches Series Design: Deborah Perdue

Layout Editor: Jill McLain

Proofreaders: Amy M. Eisenstein, MaryBeth Harnisch, Jo Alice Darden, Jill McLain, Stephen Nill

Administrative

CharityChannel LLC: Stephen C. Nill, CEO

Marketing and Public Relations: John Millen

Contents

Chapter One

Planning for a Capital Campaign

IN THIS CHAPTER

- ···→ Where will you find campaign donors?

- ···→ What are your current sources of funding?

- ···→ How many of these sources are likely to fund your campaign?

- ···→ How much "new money" is this campaign likely to generate?

Before we begin to do an in-depth assessment to determine whether your organization has the infrastructure in place to run a campaign, as well as the community awareness needed to generate excitement about your campaign, let's look at some basic planning data.

Although it is often said that a capital campaign should be able to generate anywhere from three to ten times the amount of money you raise in annual giving, it is difficult to generalize, since many factors affect the success of a campaign. Your goal will be solidified once you've done a planning study. However, it is good to reflect early in your planning on whether your expectations are realistic, so let's look at some facts:

Do you have donors who will support your campaign?

If your organization depends solely on grants for its funding, you will face challenges in finding individual donors and corporate donors to support a capital campaign. Most foundations fund programs, but only certain foundations will support capital projects. Corporations might be more likely to support a capital campaign because there will be ways to recognize the company through named-gift opportunities. Donors are the lifeblood of any campaign, so let's look at the number of donors that could potentially step up to support this effort.

The following questions will help you estimate the number of leadership donors who may be able to support your campaign:

◆ How many total donors (individuals, businesses, organizations, and private foundations) made gifts to your organization during the last twelve-month period for which this information is available, typically a fiscal and/or calendar year? _____

◆ What was the total dollar value of the *unrestricted* gifts (gifts that may be used for any purpose at your organization's discretion) your organization received last year from *individuals*? $_____

◆ What was the total dollar value of the *unrestricted* gifts your organization received last year from *businesses and organizations*? $_____

◆ What was the total dollar value of the *unrestricted* gifts your organization received last year from *foundations*? $_____

◆ What was the total dollar value of *all unrestricted* gifts your organization received last year? $_____

◆ What was the total dollar value of all *restricted-use* gifts (donations for a specific project or program that have been restricted by the donor) your organization received last year? $_____

◆ What was the total dollar value of *all gifts* from *all sources* that your organization received last year? $_____

◆ How much money do you need to raise through charitable giving to fund your organization's capital and/or endowment needs? (Enter estimated amount or actual amount if available.) $_____

◆ How many total donors (individuals, businesses, organizations, and private foundations) in your database have ever made one or more gifts of *any kind* to your organization? $_____

Named-Gift Opportunity

Within a campaign, or for other special projects, major donors will have the opportunity to name a building, a room, or an area after themselves, their companies, or loved ones, for example:

◆ The Sally Brown Library

◆ The Walter & Eleanor Smith Meditation Garden

◆ The Mega-Computer Company Technology Center

◆ How many total *prospective* donors (individuals, businesses, organizations, and private foundations) who have *never* made any gift of *any kind* to your organization are in your database (this is often the list to which you send your newsletters and other mailings)? _____

Prospective donors are often classified as suspects, prospects, and expects, depending on what the likelihood of their making a gift is determined to be after research.

Some Facts about Giving

Most charitable gifts come from individuals.
The following chart, based on *Giving USA* statistics, illustrates charitable contributions in the United States by corporations, foundations, and individuals.

Suspect: an individual, company, or foundation that you believe *might be* interested in supporting your cause

Prospect: an individual, company, or foundation that, after research, has been determined to be *likely to* support your cause

Expect: an individual, company, or foundation that, after being approached by you, has indicated they will *probably or certainly* support your cause

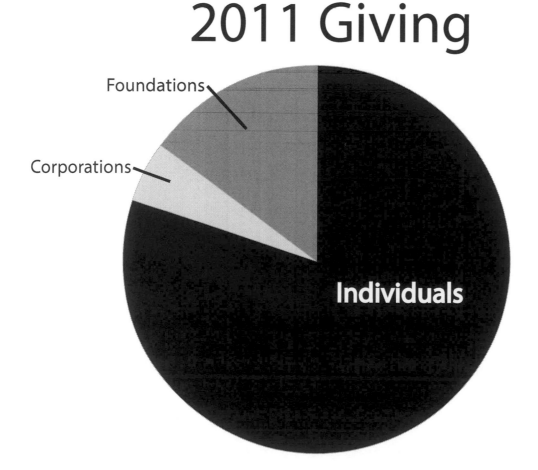

2011 Giving

During a capital campaign, these figures often shift. Many corporations tend to support capital campaigns because of the recognition opportunities involved in naming buildings, rooms, or areas. But it is wise to keep these figures in mind when determining who your capital giving prospects will be.

How does your organization stack up against these statistics?

Last year we raised a total of $_____ from the following sources:

❑ Individuals $_____

❑ Foundations $_____

❑ Businesses $_____

❑ Other $_____

Total $_____

Our pie chart looks like this:

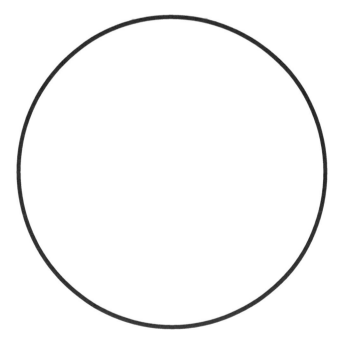

The estimated goal for our capital campaign is $_____

Ratio of annual giving to capital campaign goal ____:____, or our capital campaign goal is _____ times the total amount we raise annually.

Additional Facts to Consider

How many of the foundations that support us annually also provide capital grants?   _____

What is the typical range of these capital grants? $_____

Do we have a list of prospective individual major donors who could each give 10 percent or more of the goal?   _____

If so, how many have we identified? _____. List these prospective donors below:

_____

_____

_____

_____

_____

_____

_____

What is the largest corporate gift we have ever received? $_____

Do we have relationships with business leaders who could influence major capital gifts?

   ❑ Yes.

   ❑ No.

Who are these corporate leaders?

_____

_____

_____

_____

_____

_____

_____

What other sources can we expect to fund our campaign (churches, auxiliaries, etc.?)

_____

_____

Based on your research into current giving from various sources, try to estimate the amount of money you think you can raise from each of these sources during your capital campaign:

What percentage of our capital campaign do we expect to raise
from *foundations*?   _____ percent ($_____)

What percentage of our capital campaign do we expect to
raise from *corporations*?   _____ percent ($_____)

What percentage of our capital campaign do we expect to raise
from *other organizations*?   _____ percent ($_____)

What percentage of our capital campaign can we expect to raise
from *individuals*?   _____ percent ($_____)

                                                    Total 100 percent ($_____)

You will need to do an assessment of your current fundraising before initiating a capital
campaign. Here are some facts that should help:

The ratio of our campaign to our annual fundraising results is ____:____ ($ estimated campaign
goal: $ annual fundraising total).

Sample $350,000 annual amount raised from all sources: $7,000,000 campaign goal = 1:20 ratio.

Even if your ratio seems too high, this might not preclude a successful campaign. There are
many variables to consider; these will be discussed in this workbook. It will, however, be good
to weigh this ratio along with all the other pros and cons we will uncover in this workbook.

Number of donors we currently have:

	Individuals	Businesses Corporations	Foundations	Organizations	Government Funders	Total
Number of donors in this category						
Amount raised last year from this category						
Number of donors we believe will support our campaign						
Amount we need to raise from this source for our campaign						

To Recap

◆ Assess your current database to determine the sources of donations, amount and
percentage received from each source, and amount you expect to receive from each
source during the campaign.

◆ Review your database and categorize those in it as suspects, prospects, or expects.

◆ Review your list of potential campaign donors and determine who might need more
research and cultivation to move to the next level of interest.

Chapter Two

Donor Relations

IN THIS CHAPTER

···→ How do you cultivate new donors?

···→ How solid are your organization's relationships with existing donors?

···→ How do you define major donors for your organization?

···→ How can you improve donor relations?

Contrary to popular opinion, capital campaigns are not generally the best way to reach new donors, although often a donor will be inspired by the larger vision of your organization. Often donors who have given at minimal levels in the past have never given major gifts because you've never *asked* them for major gifts. In reality, most donations for your campaign will come from donors who already support your organization. However, you need to establish a good rapport with these donors, cultivate them well, and wait to make the ask until donors demonstrate they are ready to be asked.

Proper cultivation is especially important during a capital campaign, in which you will be asking for significant sums of money. If you don't think you have established the kind of relationships that will enable you to sit down with major donors and ask for significant investments from them, you may want to plan some cultivation activities and events before you launch your campaign. Here are some questions about your relationships with your existing donors to help you determine their readiness to support your capital campaign.

How would you characterize your organization's overall relationship with your donors?

❑ Excellent

❑ Good

❑ Okay

❑ Not so good

How frequently does someone from your organization meet individually and face-to-face with major donors and/or qualified prospective major donors (interested, supportive, capable of making large gifts), either formally or informally, to hear their views and to keep them updated about your programs, goals, and needs?

❑ Frequently: two or more times a year with almost all of them

❑ Often: at least once a year with most

❑ Fairly often: almost once a year with many

❑ Rarely: only with a few every once in a while

Kent Stroman, in the In the Trenches series book *Asking About Asking: Mastering the Art of Conversational Fundraising*, lists the ten stair steps that need to take place before you ask for a gift.

Let's talk a little more about "major donors." What does your organization consider a "major gift"? This is different for every organization; for some it could be $100, for others $100,000, or even $1,000,000. Your organization might not even have considered categorizing what constitutes a major gift. If that is the case, let's start with the 95/5 Rule.

Let's define a major gift for your organization:

We currently describe a major gift as one of $_____ or more.

The largest gift we have ever received is $_____.

The top 10 percent of our donors gave gifts ranging from $_____ to $_____ last year. The average of these gifts is $_____.

The top 5 percent of our donors gave gifts ranging from $_____ to $_____ last year. The average of these gifts is $_____.

The 95/5 Rule

You may be familiar with Pareto's Law, or what is known as the 80/20 Rule. Pareto said that 80 percent of the outputs are generally produced by 20 percent of those doing the work. When I first entered the fundraising profession, this rule was also used to describe development—80 percent of the funds that an organization received typically came from 20 percent of its donors. Over time, however, this rule morphed into the 90/10 Rule, and now, most researchers cite this rule as the 95/5 Rule. Ninety-five percent of your donations will likely come from 5 percent of your donors.

definition

The largest lifetime donor we have has given us $_____ a period of _____ years.

Based on the above information, what is a logical number for your organization to consider as a major gift? $_____

Small donors become major donors because you've developed strong relationships with them. They trust you. They know you appreciate their contributions. You connect with them. Look at your donor relations and see how your organization stacks up:

How often does your organization communicate with its constituents (newsletter, e-mail, telephone, social media, general mailing, etc.) in a manner that most recipients are *not* likely to think that your communication's main purpose is to ask for a contribution?

    ❑ Eight or more times a year

    ❑ Four to seven times a year

    ❑ Two to three times a year

    ❑ Fewer than two times per year

How many individuals, businesses, organizations, and private foundations have supported your organization financially in the past (at any level)?

❏ Ten or more

❏ Five to nine

❏ One to four

❏ Zero

How many are capable of making significant gifts and might consider supporting your campaign with contributions of at least 10 percent of the campaign's goal?

❏ Ten or more

❏ Five to nine

❏ One to four

❏ Zero

If your organization ranked low on the above questions, you will need to develop some tools to communicate with and cultivate your donors before they are willing to invest in your capital campaign. If your organization needs to do extensive cultivation and awareness-raising, it might mean delaying your campaign by a year or more.

Some things you might consider doing to communicate better with your donors are:

◆ Develop and distribute an annual report.

◆ Develop an e-newsletter that can be monitored for tracking: who opens your newsletter, how many links the recipient clicks on, and the number of people to whom the recipient forwards your newsletter. Those whom you've determined to be regular readers can be placed into the prospect pool; those who do not open your newsletter might need to be cultivated further.

◆ Conduct a board "thank-a-thon" simply to call donors, thanking them for their contributions, *without* asking them for money.

◆ Send your donors a thank-you note and tell them how their charitable gifts were used. A photo of your program in action makes the message even stronger.

◆ Use social media, such as Facebook and Twitter, to communicate with donors. You can provide campaign updates, announcements of campaign leadership appointments, and event invitations.

◆ Send a handwritten thank-you note within twenty-four hours of receiving a gift.

◆ Conduct cultivation events and activities, such as an open house, a business leaders' breakfast, or a cocktail party in the home of a campaign leader.

Internet Communications

Timely, pertinent social media posts, along with a dynamic website, can help increase your organization's standing in the community. Consider assigning a staff member or volunteer to ensure a series of regular Tweets and Facebook updates. Likewise, task a staff member, volunteer, or outside contractor with website oversight; keep the content interactive, fresh, and compelling.

Let's look at how you're doing in these areas:

Our website is up-to-date and contains all of the basic contact and programmatic information visitors would want to know about our organization, as well as interactive features, including a "Donate Now" button.

❑ Yes.

❑ No.

❑ We're working on it.

We use the following social media regularly:

❑ Facebook

❑ Twitter

❑ LinkedIn

❑ You Tube

❑ Other _____

Communications on a Shoestring Budget

You don't have to spend a lot of money to have great donor communications. Some things you can do at little or no expense:

◆ Add a PR twist to your 990 Form. Talk about your program success and provide stories about your clients. (Remember that anyone can view your 990 at www.guidestar.com.)

◆ Produce a professional-looking but low-cost annual report by including photos and stories about those you have helped. (You might ask a local business or donor to underwrite the cost of your annual report and/or include a response envelope for donations when sending it out.)

◆ Post your 990 Form and annual report on your website. This shows that your organization is transparent and communicates your success to any potential donors researching your organization.

◆ Thank donors within twenty-four hours of receiving their gifts, and remember to tell them that their gifts made a difference in the lives of those you serve.

practical tip

If you are falling short in these areas, your campaign will suffer because you will not have the "buzz" that successful campaigns find helpful in generating excitement about the project. So, let's develop a plan for better donor communications:

In the next year, we will:

- ❑ Develop or improve our annual report. This will cost $_____ and will be assigned to the following staff person: _____.

- ❑ Develop or revise our newsletter, ensure that the newsletter goes out regularly (monthly or quarterly), and clean up our mailing list. This will cost $_____ and will be assigned to the following staff person: _____.

- ❑ Develop/implement a system to monitor results of our e-newsletter. (These systems are usually free with the system you use to deliver your newsletter.) This task will be assigned to the following staff person: _____.

- ❑ Develop a "thank-a-thon" to call donors thanking them for their gifts. The level of donors we will call are those who have given a gift of $_____ or more.

This "thank-a-thon" will be done by the following date: _____. Calls will be made by:

- ❑ Staff

- ❑ Board members

- ❑ Volunteers

- ❑ Send personal thank-you notes to donors for gifts of $_____or more. The message(s) we want to send these donors will include:

_____

_____

_____

These notes will be sent within _____ hours/days of receipt of the gift by our organization. These notes will be signed by:

- ❑ Staff

- ❑ Board members

- ❑ Volunteers

Utilize social media to communicate with donors. The messages we want to send our donors include:

_____

_____

_____

The social media we will use include:

❑ Facebook

❑ Twitter

❑ LinkedIn

❑ You Tube

❑ Other _____

❑ The frequency of social media messages will be _____ times per month.

The staff person assigned to coordinate these communications strategies is: _____
_____.

Our timeline for implementing our social media strategy is _____.

Social media are becoming more prevalent in all types of fundraising and are important for nonprofits in general to spread the word about the good work being done in this sector. However, don't plan to raise big bucks by Tweeting and posting on Facebook. This is part of your overall campaign strategy, but *not* the main part.

Community Awareness

Although your relationships with your current donors are of primary importance during a campaign, there is also a great benefit to having strong awareness of your organization within the community. Considering the external factors will also be important.

A capital campaign is the most public type of fundraising your organization will do. While most of the donors to your campaign will be among your loyal supporters, a capital campaign provides you with the optimum opportunity to reach out and create awareness in the entire community. Many organizations have successfully used a campaign to attract new donors to their causes.

Below are some questions to ask about your community. Remember that your community may be local, regional, national, or international. If your campaign will be national or international, you will need to determine the geographic regions in which you have large pockets of donors and look at the economic conditions in those areas.

Describe the present state of the economy as it is probably perceived by your major donor prospects.

❑ Strong

❑ Improving

❑ Weakening

❑ Poor

How well known is your organization within the geographic area in which your program is carried out?

❑ Well known

❑ Somewhat known

❑ Hardly known

❑ All but invisible

How would you characterize the relationships your organization has with local, regional, and/or national media (whichever is most relevant to your situation)?

❑ Excellent

❑ Good

❑ Fair

❑ Poor

Overall, how strong is your organization's website?

❑ Very strong

❑ Good

❑ Needs improvement

❑ Weak or we have no website at all

Although there is little you can do about the economic climate, or even the perception of the economic climate shared by your donors, there are some things you can do to better position your organization within your community. You can strengthen your organization's brand, improve its website, and understand community perceptions of your organization.

Competition

Knowing your competition is also helpful. Although there might be numerous campaigns running simultaneously in your community, not all of these will interfere with your campaign. For example, donors might support their church or their university and still be committed to supporting your organization. However, if an organization that is in direct competition with yours is planning a capital campaign, it might be difficult for community members to justify supporting two campaigns for two organizations with similar missions.

In your community, there might be other fundraising campaigns under way that are likely to approach your best large-gift prospects. How many such campaigns are planned or are presently under way that might be viewed by your prospects as "competing" with your campaign?

❑ Many

❑ Several

❑ Maybe a few

❑ None

How can you improve your chances of standing out from the competition.

First, list other campaigns that might be happening in your community at the same time you are considering running your campaign. Which of these campaigns might be likely to share your constituency base? What are the start and end dates of these campaigns? How likely is it that your campaign will be greatly affected by this competition?

Organization running capital campaign	Organization A	Organization B	Organization C	Organization D
Goal of campaign (if known)				
This campaign is in the planning phase (or date planning phase will start, if known).				

(Continued)

Organization running capital campaign	Organization A	Organization B	Organization	Organization
This campaign is in the quiet phase (or date the quiet phase will start, if known).				
This campaign is in the public phase (or date the public phase will start, if known).				
Overlap of timing with our campaign (high, medium, or low)				
Overlap of constituents with our campaign (high, medium, or low)				

Before the campaign has been formally announced, publicity should focus on your organization's programs and accomplishments. Your campaign will be very public after the quiet phase has ended and you hold the public kick-off event. You will want to get as much media coverage as possible for your kick-off event and subsequent campaign announcements and events.

In both phases, good media relationships are important. Do you have relationships with local media outlets? What local and regional media are important in your community?

Quiet Phase: the period before the campaign is officially announced, during which leadership and major gifts are obtained

Public Phase: the period after the public launch of a campaign, during which gifts are sought from the general community

List the media in your market area:

TV: _____

_____

Radio: _____

_____

Press: _____

_____

Are these media outlets aware of your organization? If not, what strategies can you develop to create more awareness? Here are some examples:

❑ Develop a media kit. Typical media kits contain agency brochures, your agency's case for support, contact information for your organization's media relations person, press releases about your programs, and a list of agency leadership, both staff and board.

The following information should be added to our media kit:

_____

_____

This kit will be developed by the following date: _____. The staff person responsible for developing this media kit is: _____.

❑ List the individual contacts at the various media outlets to whom we need to deliver a media kit.

_____

_____

❑ List the upcoming news and public interest stories (*not* related to your campaign) for which you can develop press releases.

_____

_____

_____

You might have some great human interest stories about your organization that will attract media attention. For example:

◆ A new law affecting the people you serve could be a reason to write a letter to the editor or invite the media to cover the human side of how this law affects constituents in your community.

◆ A success story about how one of the people you serve overcame the odds to accomplish something amazing could pique the interest of the local media.

Talking to your program staff or volunteers might uncover some very intriguing success stories, too. It's time now to develop a plan to get better media coverage.

❑ List issues that affect your industry about which you can write letters to the editor or hold press conferences:

_____

_____

_____

Having good relationships with the media is important because good media coverage will be critical in getting your message out to potential donors during your campaign. You should prepare a media kit and deliver it to the media contacts personally so they know who you are and what your organization does. You know you have "arrived" when the media contact *you* for comments on hot issues in your field!

Press Releases

Remember that there might be dozens, hundreds, or thousands of nonprofits in your community, all vying for the attention of the media. To make your press releases attractive to the media, they need to:

◆ Be timely

◆ Be interesting

◆ Be concise

◆ Be unique

◆ Contain contact information

Many newspapers in larger markets will not use stories that discuss event attendance or contain photos of "big checks," etc. Small local newspapers are more likely to print these types of stories.

 practical tip

Your Website

An effective website is a critical tool for building widespread community awareness. Websites are the primary source of information about a company or organization, and people check an organization's website when they want to learn more about it.

Your website should be interactive and up-to-date and should provide basic information. One way to evaluate your website is to look at other nonprofit websites, perhaps those of your competitors or organizations similar to yours in other communities.

Start by making a list of the organizations in your community that seem to be successful at attracting donors. If you are part of a national organization, make a list of those organizations that are the largest or most similar to yours. Then set a day aside to research these websites. Use the table below to list the websites you've researched, what you like/don't like about these websites, and what you need to do to improve your website.

Name of Website	similar organization/ other nonprofit	Interactive features	Up-to-date	Basic information	Ease of making a donation	Look and feel	Special features	How does our website compare?

Which of the following steps do you need to take to improve your website?

     ❑ Improve the design and color (look and feel).

     ❑ Add more information relevant to our donors.

     ❑ Install a "donate now" feature.

     ❑ Update any outdated information.

     ❑ Add interactive features, such as "volunteer now" and "sign-up" for events.

     ❑ Add downloadable informational articles and/or brochures.

     ❑ Add basic information (addresses, phone numbers, e-mail addresses, staff bios, and board lists).

     ❑ Ensure that your 990 Form is accurate and describes your programs and activities in positive, emotionally appealing, yet practical terms.

     ❑ Add the annual report and/or 990 Form to the website.

     ❑ Other _____

Our website will be redesigned or improved by the following date:_____.
The person responsible for this project is _____.
The estimated cost for this project is $_____.

Cultivation Events and Activities

If you find that your organization has difficulty attracting a particular category of donors—individual major donors, foundations, organizations, or businesses—you might want to plan some special cultivation events and activities to help build relationships with these donors.

You will need to determine which are the best activities or events to attract donors, while at the same time not over-taxing your budget. For example, if you are seeking to build relationships with the business community, a business leader's breakfast might be a good event for you to consider. If, on the other hand, you want to build more awareness among major individual donors, you might plan a series of intimate cocktail parties in board members' or other volunteers' homes. Or you might want to meet with these donors one-on-one or invite them for a tour of your organization. Use the table below to create a donor cultivation plan:

Type of Donor	Event or Activity	Person or Team Responsible	Estimated Cost	Timeline to Complete
Foundations				
Businesses				
Organizations				
Individual Donors				

You might need to develop some materials, events, and/or activities to improve donor awareness and donor relations. The grid below will help you plan accordingly:

Program or Material	Estimated Cost	Person/Team Responsible	Timeline to Complete
Develop annual report			
Develop newsletter			
Conduct "thank-a-thon"			
Develop plan to send personal notes to donors			
Develop social media program			
Develop and distribute media kits			
Develop and distribute media releases			
Improve website			
Develop improved 990 reporting system			
Develop plan to visit major donors personally			
Develop plan for cultivation events and activities			

To Recap

◆ Public relations are important in both the quiet phase and the public phase of the campaign.

◆ During the quiet phase, emphasize your organization's programs and how they benefit the community.

◆ Once your campaign has been announced and you are in the public phase, your publicity should focus on campaign announcements, such as key leadership recruitment, major gifts received, and scheduled events.

Chapter Three

Financial Considerations

IN THIS CHAPTER

···→ Are you financially stable enough to operate the planned growth this campaign will fund?

···→ Do you have a good handle on how much money it will take to run a campaign?

···→ Do you have an established development program in place?

Financial stability is important, particularly to leadership donors. No one wants to fund a "sinking ship." If your organization is in a weak financial position, you will need to stabilize it. You'll need to have sufficient reserves to cover contingencies and up-front campaign costs. Remember that you will be seeking pledges that might not be paid in full for three to five years, and you will likely need to approach a financial institution for short-term financing or a construction loan. These financial entities will be asking tough questions to make sound business decisions about financing your organization.

Development Goals

During your last fiscal year, how did your organization's unrestricted gift income compare to your annual appeal goal?

❑ We exceeded our goal by 15 percent or more.

❑ We met or exceeded our goal by up to about 14 percent.

❑ We were within 5 percent of reaching our goal.

❑ We were more than 5 percent short of reaching our goal.

❑ We did not have a goal.

How would you characterize the role that fundraising and philanthropy play in helping your organization meet its annual operating budget and/or fulfill its mission?

> Philanthropy: love of humankind, usually expressed by an effort to enhance the well-being of humanity through personal acts of practical kindness or by financial support of a cause or causes, such as a charity, mutual aid, or assistance (service clubs, youth groups), quality of life (arts, education, environment), and religion.
> Source: *AFP Dictionary of Fundraising Terms*

❑ We conduct an ongoing and substantial fundraising program and receive philanthropic support each year. Without this income, our operations would be significantly curtailed, and fulfillment of our mission would be threatened.

❑ We conduct an ongoing fundraising program and receive philanthropic support each year. These funds represent a substantial part of our total operating revenue.

❑ We conduct organized fundraising and/or receive philanthropic support each year. These funds represent a relatively modest, but important, part of our total operating revenue.

❑ We have never conducted organized fundraising or regularly received philanthropic support that has represented a significant portion of our annual operating revenue.

Examine your organization's philanthropic culture before launching a campaign. If your organization does not place a high priority on philanthropy, development, and fundraising, it will be difficult to suddenly motivate board and staff to devote time, money, and energy to a major campaign effort. Below is a tool you can use to see how strong your organization's philanthropic culture is:

Assess Your Philanthropic Profile

1. Does your organization have a development office with at least one paid fundraising professional?

   ❑ Yes   ❑ No

2. Do experienced professionals staff your development office?

   ❑ Yes   ❑ No

3. Does your development budget include money for professional development (membership in professional organizations, conferences, and workshops, books and periodicals, etc.) for the development staff?

❑ Yes   ❑ No

4. Has your organization allocated a budget for a donor software system to manage fundraising activities?

❑ Yes   ❑ No

5. Do your organization's staff members understand the importance of the development function?

❑ Yes   ❑ No

6. Do staff members support the development office's efforts?

❑ Yes   ❑ No

7. Does your organization seek to hire development professionals who are certified (CFRE or ACFRE, FAHP, etc.)?

❑ Yes   ❑ No

8. Does your organization assist current staff in obtaining credentials?

❑ Yes   ❑ No

9. Does your chief development officer attend board meetings?

❑ Yes   ❑ No

10. Is your board committed to development (do members give and get money for the organization)?

❑ Yes   ❑ No

11. Do you have a development committee in place?

❑ Yes   ❑ No

12. Does a development officer staff the development committee?

❑ Yes   ❑ No

13. Is there clerical support for your chief development officer?

❑ Yes   ❑ No

14. Does your development staff act and look professional?

❏ Yes   ❏ No

15. Is your development office in a prominent location, and does it have a professional appearance?

❏ Yes   ❏ No

16. Does your organization support the *AFP (Association of Fundraising Professionals) Donor Bill of Rights?*

❏ Yes   ❏ No

17. Is your organization aware of and supportive of the AFP Code of Ethical Standards?

❏ Yes   ❏ No

18. Does your organization understand the importance of donor-centered fundraising?

❏ Yes   ❏ No

19. Does your organization understand that it takes time to establish a development program?

❏ Yes   ❏ No

20. Does your organization understand that building relationships with donors is the key role of the development office?

❏ Yes   ❏ No

21. Is your organization committed to work with consultants when it is appropriate to do so, and not expect staff to manage major efforts, such as a capital campaign?

❏ Yes   ❏ No

22. Is your CEO involved in fundraising?

❏ Yes   ❏ No

23. Do you involve volunteers in your fundraising program?

❏ Yes   ❏ No

Give your organization five points for each "yes" answer, and then score yourself:

◆ 100 points or more: You have a strong philanthropic profile.

◆ 75-99 points: You have a little room for improvement.

◆ 50-74 points: You should take a serious look at whether your organization is committed to philanthropy.

◆ Less than 50 points: You need some drastic reorganization of your leadership and board.

Budget

In recent years, how successful has your organization been at balancing its annual budget?

❑ We have not operated with a balanced budget for at least half of the past five to ten years and probably won't this year.

❑ During the past five to ten years, we have operated with a balanced budget at least half of the time and will again this year.

❑ We have consistently operated with a balanced budget for the past five years and will again this year, but may have had some difficulty prior to that.

❑ We will not have a deficit this year and have operated with a balanced budget for as long as anyone can recall.

Your Financial Picture in More Detail

Our annual operating budget for the organization is $_____.

Our development/fundraising goal for last year was $_____.

Our development office budget is $_____.

We met _____ percent of our fundraising goal last year.

Fundraising is _____ percent of our overall organizational budget.

Here are some warning signs that you might need some help with your financial picture. If any of these statements is true of your

Development Budget

An annual guideline against which to measure philanthropic income and fundraising expenses

definition

organization, it might be time to step back and think about your overall development program before starting a campaign:

◆ Your budget is solely dependent on fundraising, and you have no other sources of income, such as fees for services, sales of products or services, or interest from an endowment fund.

◆ You do no fundraising at all and are totally dependent on grants, contracts, and/or fees.

◆ Your development activities consist almost entirely of special events.

◆ Your development goal is established by the finance office, the executive director, or the board, with no input from the development office.

◆ Your organization has not allocated a budget for development that includes an investment in tools to help raise money, i.e., software, training, research aids, library, fundraising materials, consultants, staff salaries, and benefits.

Many times a full-blown development audit is called for before entering into a capital campaign. At minimum, you should engage an outside consultant to do your planning study. The consultant will typically include some type of internal assessment in the study process. However, you should also try to assess some of your strengths and weaknesses internally even before engaging a consultant to do an audit.

Development audit: an objective evaluation of an organization's internal development procedures and results, usually conducted by a professional fundraising consultant.

Sometimes before a campaign, it is wise to conduct a full-scale development audit, engaging an outside consultant to do a thorough assessment of your organization's development program. If you are planning a development audit, be sure to get quotes for consultant fees so you can budget accordingly for this process.

At minimum, during the planning study process, make sure your consultant does an internal assessment before conducting the external assessment portion of the study.

In the meantime, you can do some things yourself to assess your development program. This assessment, whether done internally or by engaging an outside consultant, should help you create an integrated development plan that allows you to coordinate the campaign with other fundraising efforts. Remember that you still need to maintain your annual fundraising efforts during a campaign. A solid development plan, similar to a good campaign plan, will involve diversifying your funding streams by approaching various constituencies using a variety of fundraising methods.

You should also plan to establish a realistic goal for your annual fundraising efforts during the course of your capital campaign. Often, annual giving will be negatively impacted by the campaign because some people will choose to eliminate their annual support while they are paying their campaign pledges. With proper planning, you can keep this annual loss to a minimum. The good news is that once the campaign is over, you should see a rise in annual giving. Plan for assessing the performance of your previous fundraising activities before launching your campaign:

The person responsible for this assessment is _____. The assessment will be completed by the following date _____.
This assessment will involve an expense of $_____.

Develop realistic budgets for both the organization and the development office. The person responsible for developing these budgets is _____.
This will be accomplished by _____. We need the following information or help to do this:

_____

_____

_____

Establish realistic fundraising goals with the input of the development staff. Increase or maintain our fundraising income at a level of $_____ for the next fiscal year.

Develop a plan for raising the money to meet this goal. This plan will be developed by the following date _____. The person responsible for developing this plan is _____. We need the following information or help to develop this plan:

_____

_____

_____

You might need to bring your organizational budget in line and/or create a campaign budget. The finance department should get involved early in your campaign planning to ensure that your budget is sufficient to cover short-term costs while you are raising money.

On the development side of your organization, it might be time to conduct a development audit and create or improve your development plan to improve your philanthropic profile.

Plan to do these things:

Task	Budget	Person/Team Responsible	Timeline to Complete
Develop a more realistic organizational budget			
Assess our philanthropic profile			
Develop a campaign budget			
Conduct a development audit			
Create a development plan			
Establish a realistic plan to incorporate the campaign into our overall development efforts			

To Recap

◆ Make sure your organization is financially stable before launching a capital campaign.

◆ Develop a realistic campaign budget that is incorporated into your development office budget and your organization's budget.

◆ Examine your overall development efforts and develop a strategy to incorporate the campaign into your development plan.

Chapter Four

Mission, Vision, and Planning

IN THIS CHAPTER

- ···→ Are your mission, vision, and values statements appropriate, in written form, and clearly understood by your constituents?

- ···→ Do you have a strategic plan in place?

- ···→ Do you have a compelling case for support?

Thorough planning is critical to campaign success. Your campaign plan should emerge from your organization's overall strategic plan. During the strategic planning process, if you've identified a real need for growth, a campaign is the most logical outgrowth of this need.

You should also have an organization case for support in place from which the campaign case statement will evolve. If these things are not already in place, consider engaging your staff and board in a strategic planning process.

Perception of Your Organization

Is your organization generally perceived as having a history of doing a good job?

- ❑ Our organization has always been generally perceived as effective in how it fulfills its mission.

- ❑ Though it has not always been the case, our organization is now generally perceived as effective in how it fulfills its mission.

❑ Our organization is generally perceived as one that sporadically fulfills its mission and/or meets its goals, or we are so new that we have no real track record by which to be measured.

❑ Our organization is generally perceived as one that has often not fulfilled its potential and/or met its goals.

Your organization's mission, vision, and values will be important in developing a campaign case statement. The need for funding must relate to the needs of the community, not simply to organizational needs. Your mission, vision, and values will help prospective donors understand how you serve your community and how this campaign will help achieve a community-wide vision.

Before writing your case statement, answer these questions:

◆ What is our mission? _____.

◆ What are our values? _____.

◆ What is our vision? _____.

Is our mission concise (usually one or two sentences), and does it tell the public what we actually do?

❑ Yes.

❑ No.

❑ We're working on it.

Is our vision truly farsighted and focused externally on the community, rather than internally on our organization?

❑ Yes.

❑ No.

❑ We're working on it.

Are our values clear, and will they resonate with our potential donors?

❑ Yes.

❑ No.

❑ We're working on it.

What values do we hold near and dear? What are our "lines in the sand" on which we will not compromise?

_____

_____

_____

_____

_____

_____

You might want to plan a board and staff retreat to develop, affirm, or revise your mission, vision, and values.

How accurately does your mission statement reflect the reality of your organization's sense of purpose and its programs?

❑ Accurately; it needs no revision.

❑ Reasonably accurately; it could use fine-tuning.

❑ Not very accurately; it needs to be re-written.

❑ We don't have a mission statement.

How accurately does your vision statement reflect the reality of your organization's sense of the ideal community and its role in achieving this ideal?

❑ Accurately; it needs no revision.

❑ Reasonably accurately; it could use fine-tuning.

❑ Not very accurately; it needs to be re-written.

❑ We don't have a vision statement.

How accurately does your values statement reflect your organization's sense of the things it holds dear, the things about which you will not compromise?

❑ Accurately; it needs no revision.

❑ Reasonably accurately; it could use fine-tuning.

❑ Not very accurately; it needs to be re-written.

❑ We don't have a values statement.

Planning

Describe the process by which your organization developed its long-range (three years or more) or strategic plan:

> Strategic plan: decisions and actions that shape and guide an organization while emphasizing the future implications of present decisions. This plan usually employs a SWOT analysis (strengths, weaknesses, opportunities, and threats).
>
> **definition**

❑ It is a formal process led by an outside third party that involved both the board and senior staff, who developed the written plan.

❑ It is a process led by staff and/or board who created the written plan.

❑ It is a written plan developed by staff.

❑ There is no written long-range plan.

How long has it been since your organization formally reviewed its long-range (three years or more) plan?

❑ It has been less than sixteen months.

❑ It has been sixteen to twenty-four months.

❑ It has been more than twenty-four months.

❑ We have no long-range plan.

How would you describe your organization's current public relations/marketing plan?

❑ It is well developed, clearly understood, and implemented.

❑ It is well developed, but not being implemented as planned.

❑ It is partially developed and/or not being implemented well.

❑ We have no marketing plan.

Case for Support

Before you can develop a campaign case statement, your organization should have an overall case for support. The overall case describes your organization's mission, vision, values, plans, needs, and the opportunities for readers of the case to participate in your organization's vision. It forms the basis for a more specific campaign case statement that will focus on the need for this project in your community. It is important that your campaign case statement be developed first in a preliminary form. This preliminary case will then be tested with your constituents to see whether it is compelling enough to inspire donors to support your campaign.

How fully developed is the written case for your organization's anticipated fundraising campaign?

❑ We have a fully developed, preliminary case statement that succinctly describes our organization, its mission, and the purposes (including budgets) for which the campaign would be raising funds. Our case describes the benefits to be derived by those we serve.

> Case for Support: The case for support is the comprehensive document that describes your organization, it mission, vision, and programs. The case defines how you will solve a community problem and offers opportunities for the donor to participate in this solution. The case is the source document for all written and electronic campaign materials.
>
>

❑ We are actively developing, or have the information necessary to begin developing, a written preliminary case statement incorporating the above elements.

❑ Our organization's goals and objectives and planning relative to a campaign are not yet adequate to begin writing a preliminary case statement.

❑ We are not sure what the preliminary campaign case statement includes or involves.

How readily do you expect that your organization's constituents/supporters will understand and be motivated by the benefits to be realized by completing this project?

❑ They already understand and in fact have been seeking this project for some time. They perceive that it is addressing an urgent need.

❑ The need and benefits will be obvious to them when they hear the facts and plans.

❑ While some will understand quickly when they've heard "the case," many will need to hear it explained repeatedly.

❑ The benefits of this project will be difficult for most to grasp. It will take a long period of educating and answering questions.

How would you describe the process by which your organization decided on this project?

❑ Our members/constituents/traditional supporters have been asking for some time that this project proceed to meet a widely acknowledged need/opportunity. The decision was virtually automatic and is almost universally popular.

❑ Leaders of our organization, both volunteers and staff, participated in a comprehensive planning process that led them to adopt this project as a high priority.

❑ A strongly felt and persuasive case for the project was presented by a staff member or volunteer to a small group, and we have decided to give it a try.

❑ Growing out of some generalized discussion, some of us thought it was time to take on a major campaign.

In how much detail are you currently able to describe the physical (capital) or endowment project and the relative importance and costs of key components?

❑ Highly detailed, written descriptions of the project's various components and their costs are in-hand and if/as appropriate, we are able to answer questions about the relative importance and/or priority of the components.

❑ We have a pretty good idea of what the project will include, but written descriptions and any prioritization of its specific features have not yet been accomplished.

❑ We currently have only a generalized idea about what the project will include.

❑ We are considering several options, but have not yet determined the best route to take.

❑ We're not yet sure what we want to do.

How did you arrive at your total construction cost?

❑ After receiving our approval of the project's broad specifications, an architect provided a realistic estimate of the total cost of completing the project.

❑ A contractor, or someone experienced with similar projects such as the one we are considering, provided us with a ballpark estimate.

❑ We have heard about the costs of projects that seem similar to the one we are considering and are guessing that this is probably a good first estimate for our project.

❑ The number is based mostly on what some of us think we might be able to raise in support of the project.

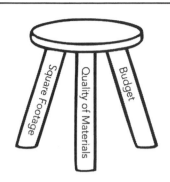

Architects often describe the building process as a three-legged stool: one leg is the square footage of the building; the second leg is the quality of materials to be used; the final leg is cost. In other words, if you have a specific number of square feet that will be required in your building and a limited budget, this will determine the quality of materials you can put into your project. Any two of the three legs will determine the third leg's results.

practical tip

Hard construction costs are not the only expenses you need to consider when budgeting for your project. Some of the soft costs include:

◆ Legal fees

◆ Architects' and engineering fees

◆ Environmental impact and/or planning department fees

◆ Inflation of construction estimates

◆ Contingencies

◆ New furnishings (often referred to as FF&E—furniture, fixtures, and equipment)

◆ New communications systems

◆ Short-term loans to cover cash flow shortages

To what extent does your currently envisioned campaign goal provide for these expenses:

❑ All or most of these items have been carefully reviewed and budgeted appropriately.

❑ Many of these items have been reviewed and budgeted appropriately.

❑ Some of these items have been reviewed and budgeted.

❑ None has yet been reviewed for possible inclusion in the budget.

Let's discuss your organization's strategic plan. If you've gone through the strategic planning process recently, the following components are probably in place. If not, you might need to work on your strategic plan. Carefully review the following list and determine what you need to have in place in your organization before you can start to plan a campaign:

❑ We need to update our mission statement.

❑ We need to develop or update our vision statement.

❑ We need to develop or update our values statement.

❑ We need to create or update a strategic plan.

❑ We need a marketing plan.

❑ We need a development plan.

❑ We need to obtain architectural drawings and costs for our project.

❑ We need to develop a preliminary case for support.

❑ We need to conduct a planning (feasibility) study.

Our mission statement is:

_____

_____

_____

_____

We feel this mission statement is:

❑ Too long

❑ Too short

❑ The right length

The content of this mission statement is:

❑ Excellent as is

❑ Good, but needs some improvement

❑ Poor because:

❑ It's jargon-filled and/or contains over-used phrases.

❑ It's irrelevant to what we actually do.

❑ It's not comprehensive.

❑ It's too wordy.

❑ It does not evoke passion in the reader.

Often a good exercise to help refine your mission is to review websites or other sources of mission statements for other nonprofits.

❑ We have reviewed other mission statements.

❑ We have not done this exercise, but will do it now.

Once you've reviewed some other mission statements, which ones stand out as being well written?

_____

_____

_____

_____

What do you like about these mission statements?

_____

_____

_____

What do you like about your mission statement?

_____

_____

_____

What don't you like about your mission statement?

_____

_____

_____

We will take the following steps to improve our mission statement:

❑ Engage the board and senior staff in a mission statement revision process

❑ Engage an outside consultant to direct this process

Our revised mission statement will be developed by the following date _____.
The person responsible for coordinating this effort is _____.
The budget for this process is $_____.

Our vision statement is:

_____

_____

_____

_____

We feel this vision statement is:

❑ Too long

❑ Too short

❑ The right length

The content of this vision statement is:

❑ Excellent as is

❑ Good, but needs some improvement

❑ Poor because:

   ❑ It's jargon-filled and/or contains over-used phrases.

   ❑ It's not comprehensive.

   ❑ It's too wordy.

   ❑ It does not evoke passion in the reader.

   ❑ It does not really address how we see our organization and/or our community ten or more years from now.

   ❑ We don't have a vision statement at all.

As with the mission statement, a good exercise to help refine your vision is to review websites or other sources of vision statements for other nonprofits.

❏ We have reviewed other vision statements.

❏ We have not done this exercise, but will do it now.

Once you've reviewed some other vision statements, which ones stand out as being well written?

_____

_____

_____

What do you like about these vision statements?

_____

_____

_____

What do you like about your vision statement?

_____

_____

_____

What don't you like about your vision statement?

_____

_____

_____

We will take the following steps to improve our vision statement:

❏ Engage the board and senior staff in a vision statement revision process

❏ Engage an outside consultant to direct this process

Our revised vision statement will be developed by the following date _____.
The person responsible for coordinating this effort is _____.
The budget for this process is $_____.

Our values statement is:

_____

_____

_____

_____

We feel this values statement is:

❑ Too long

❑ Too short

❑ The right length

The content of this values statement is:

❑ Excellent as is

❑ Good, but needs some improvement

❑ Poor because:

  ❑ It's jargon-filled and/or contains over-used phrases.

  ❑ It's not comprehensive.

  ❑ It's too wordy.

  ❑ It does not evoke passion in the reader.

  ❑ It does not really address the values our organization feels strongly about.

  ❑ We don't have a values statement at all.

Often, a good exercise to help refine your values is to review a list of ideals. Use the list in the sidebar as a starting point for your organization to develop its values statement.

❑ We have reviewed a list of values.

❑ We have not done this exercise, but will do it now.

Sample Values:

Authenticity	Dependability	Originality	Trustworthiness
Accountability	Diversity	Integrity	Truth
Balance	Daring	Initiative	Uniqueness
Caring	Efficiency	Listening	Wellness
Credentials	Effectiveness	Natural	
Compassion	Fairness	Pride	
Confidence	Freedom	Responsibility	
Conviction	Honesty	Security	

Example

Once you've reviewed the list of values, which ones seem appropriate for your organization?

_____

_____

_____

What do you like about these new values?

_____

_____

_____

What do you like about your current values statement?

_____

_____

_____

What don't you like about your current values statement?

_____

_____

_____

We will take the following steps to improve our values statement:

❑ Engage the board and senior staff in a values statement revision process

❑ Engage an outside consultant to direct this process

Our revised values statement will be developed by the following date _____.
The person responsible for coordinating this effort is _____.
The budget for this process is $_____.

Planning

Organizational planning is critical. If you don't have solid plans, it will be difficult to attract funders. Remember that while emotion can draw donors to your organization, serious donors want to know that you can deliver on your promises and that your plan clearly makes sense for your organization *and* for the community. I generally recommended that you have outside facilitators help with strategic planning and sometimes other plans, as well.

How does your organization rate in planning?

We need to develop the following:

❑ A strategic plan encompassing all areas of the organization

❑ A program plan describing anticipated growth or decline in program areas, personnel requirements, and user groups

❑ A facility plan that describes the buildings, equipment, and other capital investments we need to operate our programs

❑ A financial plan explaining how we will finance our programs and facilities and how we will invest our money

❑ A development plan that details how we will raise the money to operate the organization

❑ A marketing plan that describes how we will approach stakeholders, including donors and users of our services

❑ A human resource plan that includes staff, board, and volunteers

The missing plans will be developed by the following date(s) _____.
The person(s) responsible for developing the plan(s)is/are.

_____

_____

The budget for developing these plans, including the use of outside consultants, is
$_____.

If your campaign involves new construction, expansion of existing facilities, or renovation of an existing building(s), you will need to do an architectural study of your existing facilities or have an architect draw up plans for the new building.

So where do you stand with the plans for your new facility?

☐ We have land/buildings and have engaged an architect.

☐ We need to find land on which to build.

☐ We have studied the feasibility of expansion/renovation.

☐ We have a construction manager in place.

☐ We need to find an architect and/or a construction manager.

If you need to purchase land, you should work with a real estate agent to help with this process. If you are in the market for land, do you have a professionally developed plan for how much land you need and what your requirements for this land are (i.e., proximity to bus lines, number of acres, convenient location)?

☐ Yes.

☐ No.

If you do not have land, complete the steps you need to acquire land:

We will have a plan for the land requirements by the following date _____.
The person responsible for developing this plan is _____.
The budget for this land acquisition is $_____.

If you already have land and/or buildings you are renovating/expanding, complete the steps you need to develop a building plan:

We will engage an architect by the following date _____. The architectural firms we are considering are _____. The person(s) responsible for engaging an architect is/are _____
_____.
The budget for pre-construction architectural services is $_____.

Developing Your Case for Support

You will want to develop a preliminary case for support to test before launching your capital campaign with a fully developed case statement. Sometimes what *you* might think is important is not what community members feel is important. Based on feedback, your case might need to be modified after it's been tested. Goals might need to be adjusted if the community does not think your goal is realistic. Is your organization ready to test your case?

❑ We have a preliminary case for support written by a development professional.

❑ We plan to engage a consultant to do the planning/feasibility study, and that person will write the case for support.

Our case for support will be written by the following date _____. The person responsible for writing the case is _____. The budget for preparing the case is $_____ or is included in the budget for the planning/feasibility study.

You might need to work on your planning for the campaign and/or your overall organization planning. Use the table below to develop a strategy:

Planning Task	Budget	Person or Team Responsible	Timeline to Complete
Purchase land			
Develop architectural plans			
Develop a case for support			
Create, affirm, or refine mission statement			
Create, affirm, or revise vision statement			
Create, affirm, or revise values statement			
Develop a strategic plan			
Develop a facilities plan			
Develop a financial plan			
Develop a program plan			

To Recap

◆ Your campaign should evolve from your strategic planning process.

◆ You need an overall plan for the organization that guides and directs every aspect of your organization, including programs, facilities, finance, and human resources.

◆ You will need both an overall organization case for support and a campaign case statement.

◆ Your case should include a realistic budget for the project.

Chapter Five

The Planning Study

IN THIS CHAPTER

····➔ What is a planning study, and do you need one?

····➔ Who should do the study?

····➔ When are you ready for the study?

In most cases, you will want to do a planning study (sometimes called a feasibility study) before you decide to proceed with a campaign. The study should be done by a consultant to ensure that the people being interviewed feel comfortable talking about their perceptions of your organization. An experienced consultant will know not only how to ask the right questions, but also how to analyze the results of the interviews and make recommendations for your campaign.

A planning study will generally take between three and six months to complete, and the costs will depend on the size of your constituency base, the geographic scope of the study interview process, and other factors. You should expect a full report from the consultant with recommendations for a campaign goal and timeline, the availability of major donors for your campaign, and any issues that might affect the success of your campaign. Conducting a study will help you prepare for a successful campaign, but is not the *only* factor in determining success.

What is your organization's position relative to conducting a formal campaign feasibility/ planning study?

❑ We plan to contract with an experienced professional consultant to conduct a study for us.

❑ We will probably have staff and/or volunteer leaders perform an analysis of our potential.

❑ We haven't considered whether we need to conduct a study.

❑ We think we know our situation well enough that we don't need to conduct a study.

The people to be interviewed during this study will usually be major donors to your organization, those who you feel could be major donors, and those with broad community connections who might be willing to serve on the campaign cabinet. Before engaging a consultant to do the study, you should attempt to determine whom you will ask the consultant to interview. Most consultants will want to interview between thirty and fifty people. If your campaign is larger in size and scope, this number could be greater. Not all of the people on your list will be available for an interview, so you should start with a list of seventy-five to one hundred people. The list will then be divided into an A List, a B List, and a C List. A-list people are those who *must* be interviewed; B-list individuals are those who *should* be interviewed; and the C list contains the names of those who *could* be interviewed.

> A planning or feasibility study is the process by which an organization determines the feasibility of its campaign. This includes:
>
> ◆ The likelihood that the goal can be reached
>
> ◆ An analysis of donor availability identifying who will support the project at the necessary levels
>
> ◆ The availability of leadership-level volunteers to serve on the campaign cabinet
>
> The study is done by an experienced outside consultant who will interview prospective supporters, analyze the results of the interviews, and make recommendations for the campaign goal and timeline.
>
>

Do you have a list of prospective interviewees?

❑ We have developed a list of people to be interviewed during the study. There are _____ (number of people) on this list.

   ❑ We have divided this list by prioritizing those to be interviewed into A, B, and C Lists.

❑ We do not have a list developed, but can put one together fairly quickly.

❑ We have no idea whom we should plan to interview and will need some guidance from the consultant in this regard.

Some people who will be on our A List include:

_____

_____

_____

_____

_____

_____

_____

_____

_____

_____

_____

_____

_____

Engaging a Consultant for the Study

If you have not yet identified a consultant for the study, how will you go about this process?

❑ We have identified a consultant who will perform the study.

❑ We have identified the following firms/consultants to be interviewed:

_____

_____

❏ We will ask for written proposals from these consultants by the following date _____.

The person(s) responsible for developing the request for proposal (RFP), reviewing these proposals, and making recommendations to the board is/are _____ _____ _____.

Sources to Help You Find a Consultant

AFP Consultant Directory: www.afpnet.org

CharityChannel Consultants Registry Online: www.charitychannel.com

👍 practical tip

We will interview selected firms/consultants by the following date: _____.
The persons responsible for interviewing consultants are: _____.

We will make the selection and notify the preferred consultant/firm by the following date _____. The person responsible for notifying the selected firm is _____. The person responsible for preparing the consulting contract is _____.

The consultant/firm who will conduct our planning study is _____.
The study will be completed by the following date _____ _____. The budget for the study is $_____.

You will most likely want to conduct a study before launching your campaign. This grid will help you develop a plan to do the study:

Planning Study Task	Budget	Person or Team Responsible	Timeline to Complete
Determine need for study			
Establish goals of study			
Develop list of consultants to be considered			
Develop RFP			
Distribute RFP			
Select consultants to be interviewed			
Interview consultants			
Select consultant			
Sign contract			

To Recap

◆ You will want to conduct a planning (feasibility) study to assess both your internal readiness for a campaign and the community's willingness and ability to support this campaign.

◆ The study should be conducted by an outside consultant who will have the skills, experience, and expertise to develop the questions to be asked, interview prospective donors, analyze the results of the interview, and make recommendations for your campaign.

◆ You can facilitate the study process by assembling the material needed for the case for support and a list of people to be interviewed.

Chapter Six

Executive Leadership Experience

IN THIS CHAPTER

····→ What role does your CEO play in the campaign?

····→ How do you involve the entire staff in the campaign?

····→ Once you've done the study, do you need a consultant to help run the campaign?

Your organization's CEO will have an important role to play in the campaign, as will the development staff and other staff members in your organization. In particular, the development staff and the CEO will need to clear their schedules to devote sufficient time to the campaign. In many cases, temporary staff might be needed to manage the campaign. Even with a top-notch staff, a consultant is generally engaged to provide the specialized skills a campaign requires. A consultant helps ensure that campaign timelines are met.

Executive Leadership

The CEO's role in your campaign is critical. It is essential that your CEO is willing and able to devote sufficient time to the process of identifying, cultivating, and soliciting donors. It is also be important for the CEO to motivate and inspire campaign leaders. And, of course, the CEO is expected to make an early financial commitment to the campaign to inspire others to get on board.

How long has your organization's senior executive officer been with your organization (in any capacity)?

❑ Eight years or more

❑ Three to seven years

❑ Less than three years

❑ Position is vacant or does not exist.

If your CEO unexpectedly leaves in the middle of a campaign, the effects can be detrimental. Even if the departure has been planned, it can send the wrong message to your donors. It is critical to have a succession plan in place, and if the departure involves a termination of the CEO for cause, a crisis plan might be needed.

Answer these questions about the tenure of your CEO:

❑ Our CEO will remain CEO for the duration of the campaign.

❑ Our CEO is likely to retire or leave the organization before this campaign is completed.

❑ We have a succession plan in place if our CEO leaves during the campaign.

If we need to develop a succession plan, the person(s) responsible for this plan is/are _____. We will develop this plan by the following date _____. The budget for developing this plan is $_____.

Does your CEO need to be educated in capital campaigns and the role of the CEO in a campaign?

❑ Yes.

❑ No.

We will engage the following person/firm to provide this education _____ _____. This education will be completed by the following date _____. The budget for this education is $_____.

If you asked your CEO to recite your organization's mission statement, how accurate would it be?

❑ Perfectly

❑ Very close

❑ Not well

❑ Couldn't do it or don't have one

How do you perceive the fundraising comfort level of your senior executive officer?

❑ Obviously very comfortable; enjoys asking for financial support and seeks opportunities to do so

❑ Seems comfortable; readily accepts and performs fundraising responsibilities, including solicitations, effectively

❑ Seems uncomfortable; rarely participates in direct solicitation activities, even with the organization's most important prospects

❑ Very uncomfortable; will not participate in face-to-face solicitations

Is your CEO aware of the need for, and committed to, allocating 50 percent or more of the work week to the campaign?

❑ Yes.

❑ No.

❑ Haven't discussed this yet, but we believe our CEO is willing to do whatever it takes.

Staff Engagement

Your organization's entire staff should be informed of the campaign early in the planning phase. It will be important to have your staff support the campaign financially and otherwise, again, to show the community that your organization is *truly* committed to this campaign.

If you have not been conducting an annual staff appeal, some of these questions may result in negative answers. Don't despair—this campaign is a perfect time to introduce staff giving to your organization. Leaders at nonprofit organizations often feel that it is inappropriate to invite the staff to participate financially in fund drives. However, employees of nonprofits are generally committed to the organizations for which they work and should be provided an opportunity to show their commitment by participating in campaigns and other fundraising appeals.

What percentage of senior staff made a financial contribution to your organization last year?

❑ 100 percent

❑ At least 50 percent, but fewer than 100 percent

Staff Appeal

Conducting an ongoing annual staff appeal helps employees feel they are part of your organization's success. It also helps lay the groundwork for a campaign. Offering payroll deduction is a great way to encourage staff members to support your organization.

 practical tip

❑ At least 25 percent, but fewer than 50 percent

❑ Fewer than 25 percent

The Consultant's Role in Your Campaign

Once your study is completed, you will need to decide whether a consultant is needed to help implement the campaign, and if so, exactly what role the consultant will play. These roles vary and typically include:

◆ Resident counsel, in which the consultant will be at your organization daily for a specific period, usually months or perhaps years

◆ Retainer, in which a consultant is retained for a specified number of days per month to provide general guidance for the campaign

◆ Project-based consulting, in which a consultant is engaged to complete specific tasks, could include preparing the case for support, creating the campaign plan, writing grant proposals for the campaign, training volunteers, or other tasks related to the campaign

Some questions you might want to ask before you decide to engage counsel include:

Has your organization worked with a fundraising consultant in the last five years?

❑ Yes, in a substantial and significant manner

❑ Yes, in a relatively minor way

❑ No

How was your organization's most recent experience working with a fundraising consultant?

❑ Excellent

❑ Good

❑ Unsatisfactory

❑ Have not worked with one

Has your organization engaged a fundraising consultant for this campaign?

❑ Yes

❑ Interviewing consultants now

❑ No, but we plan to

❑ Don't plan to engage a consultant

If you have already conducted a planning study, you will most likely have an idea of how you will utilize consulting services during the campaign. If not, you will need to talk to consultants about the types of services they can offer.

Most organizations hire a consultant when considering a campaign because they don't have the time, expertise, or knowledge to run a campaign on their own. You need to understand what a consultant can and cannot do for you. If you think a consultant is the magic bullet you need to land those big gifts, that is not the case. It is *not* the consultant's job to raise money for you.

Think about how you would feel if a consultant you did not know came to you and asked for a gift. Wouldn't you respond better to someone in your community whom you know and respect? Someone who is contributing at the same level at which you are being asked to contribute? Asking is the role of people inside the organization, preferably volunteers, rather than consultants.

> It's important to understand what a consultant *doesn't* do for you. Consultants *do not* raise the money for you. A consultant is like the coach on the football team, and volunteers are like the players; just as players run plays with the ball, volunteers will be making the ask with donors.
>
>  practical tip

Hiring a consultant is never a guarantee that your campaign will succeed. Sometimes organizations disregard basic rules of campaigning, regardless of their consultant's input. And sometimes, an organization chooses a consultant who is just not the right match for the organization or who does not have enough campaign experience.

Many times, the objectivity, creativity, knowledge, and expertise a consultant can bring to the campaign can start your organization off on the right foot. If your budget is limited, you should hire a consultant early in the process to do your study and prepare a campaign plan. The consultant might be able to tell you how you can manage a campaign on your own or with limited consulting help, once a solid plan is in place. Often, with a good plan in hand and some training and coaching by a consultant, staff can step in and manage the campaign.

> ### What a Consultant Can Do for You
>
> Consultants provide a breadth and depth of experience in campaigning and often bring creativity, energy, and an objective viewpoint to your leadership, staff, and volunteers. A consultant can say things to board members, CEOs, and volunteers that sometimes a development officer cannot. The consultant helps keep everyone on track and hold staff and volunteers' "feet to the fire."
>
>  practical tip

We believe we will need:

❑ Resident counsel (consultant), who will be on-site for a period of _____ months at an estimated cost of $ _____

❑ Full-service counsel who will not be on-site for the duration of the campaign, but will be on a monthly retainer estimated to be $_____

❑ Counsel to provide the following services: _____
_____
_____at an estimated cost of $_____

These fees will be:

❑ Included in our campaign goals

❑ Financed through our operating budget

❑ Financed through (list other sources): _____
_____.

Most organizations include the campaign costs in the overall campaign goal. However, if your organization has planned far enough in advance, you might be able to fund the campaign budget through your operating budget. This can be attractive to donors because the money raised in the campaign will go directly to the project.

Your leadership staff must play an important role in the campaign. You will most likely want to engage a consultant to help with the campaign and assist in educating your leadership staff. Let's make a plan to accomplish this:

Task	Budget	Person or Team Responsible	Timeline to Complete
Conduct an annual staff appeal			
Educate staff and leadership in campaign theory and practice			
Develop a staff training program			
Engage campaign counsel			
Develop a plan to communicate with the entire staff about the campaign plans			

To Recap

◆ The CEO and development staff will need to clear their schedules to devote time to the campaign.

◆ All staff members should be made aware of the campaign and feel engaged in the campaign process.

◆ Most organizations contract with a campaign consultant to help ensure that the campaign is successful.

Chapter Seven

Development Staff

IN THIS CHAPTER

···→ Does your staff have campaign experience?

···→ Is your staff free from over-involvement in non-development areas?

···→ Will you need to hire additional staff members to run the campaign?

The role of the development staff in your capital campaign should not be underestimated. Although not every organization will have a development staff with campaign experience, it is critical that staff can devote sufficient time to the campaign. If your staff is over-involved in planning and managing special events or writing grant proposals or involved in non-development activities, such as programs, finance, or public relations, the campaign will suffer.

The Role of the Development Staff

Let's look at the ability of your staff to launch a campaign. The answers to these questions will help you determine what kind of help you will need from a consultant.

Our development staff has campaign experience:

❑ Yes.

❑ No.

We will engage the following person/firm to provide education/training for our development staff: _____. This education will be completed by the following date _____. The budget for this education is $_____.

We will purchase the following tools (books, webinars, conferences, and seminars) to help train our development staff _____. The purchase of these tools will be completed by the following date _____. The budget for these tools is $_____.

Staffing Information

Number of full-time equivalent (FTEs) development (fundraising) staff members in your organization: _____

Number of senior staff (executive leadership) members in your organization:

_____

How long has your organization's senior development (fundraising) officer been with your organization (in any capacity)?

❏ Five years or more

❏ Three to four years

❏ Two years or less

❏ Position is vacant or does not exist.

Have you thought about who will manage the day-to-day campaign operation? If your development office is staffed by volunteers or is an office with limited staff, you will likely need additional help to manage the campaign. Even if you plan to engage a consultant, many clerical details will need to be managed, such as:

◆ Entering pledges and gifts into the database

◆ Researching donor history

◆ Sending meeting notices and minutes to campaign volunteers

◆ Generating campaign reports

◆ Communicating with the staff and volunteers about campaign progress

◆ Preparing campaign materials

◆ Generating direct mail during the later stages of the campaign

Campaign Assignments: What Can You Do Internally?

When do you need to hire a consultant or extra staff?

Activity	Skills Needed	Who in Our Organization Can Do This?	Hire a Consultant or Staff Member for:
Organize/define campaign goals and objectives	◆ Management and planning skills ◆ Knowledge of community needs ◆ Knowledge of organization's needs		
Organize/prepare schedules and guidelines	◆ Management/planning skills ◆ Budgeting skills ◆ Fundraising experience ◆ Campaign experience		
Write case statement	◆ Knowledge of organization ◆ Knowledge of the project ◆ Writing skills ◆ Understanding of psychology of philanthropy ◆ Knowledge of fundraising techniques		
Write and distribute campaign literature	◆ Writing skills ◆ Knowledge of graphic arts/printing ◆ Direct/bulk mail experience ◆ Marketing skills		
Recruit, train, and motivate volunteers	◆ Community contacts ◆ Leadership qualities ◆ Previous experience working with volunteers ◆ Group motivation experience ◆ Education training ◆ Knowledge of fundraising techniques		
Solicit prospects	◆ Knowledge of the community ◆ Communication skills ◆ Understanding of psychology of philanthropy ◆ Financial commitment to campaign		
Keep records and write reports	◆ Administrative skills ◆ Knowledge of campaign software ◆ Accounting skills ◆ Writing skills		
Handle campaign publicity	◆ Understanding of media requirements ◆ Communication skills ◆ Organizational/planning skills		

If you do not have someone who can handle these tasks, you have several options:

◆ Assign a non-development staff person to do them (who will most likely need some training).

◆ Ask your consultant to provide support services.

◆ Hire a temporary staff person to help with the campaign.

If you are planning to assign a staff person to the campaign, you need to think hard about what you can shift from this person's regular workload. If this staff member is torn between campaign activities and other familiar, more comfortable duties, it is easy to imagine which duties will be pushed aside!

Here are some steps to help you develop a plan for managing your campaign:

❑ We have someone in-house who can manage the campaign. That person is _____ _____. This person's regular duties will be handled during the campaign by _____.

❑ We will ask our consultant to manage the daily operations of the campaign. That consultant is _____. The costs to manage the campaign (in addition to consulting fees) will be $_____.

❑ We will hire a temporary staff person for _____ hours per week for _____ weeks/ months/years at an estimated cost of $_____ weekly/monthly/annually.

Is Your Staff Over-extended?

Rate your development staff's overall ability to meet its existing responsibilities:

❑ Excellent

❑ Good

❑ Not very good

❑ No development staff

Staff Education and Training

It is important that your organization understand the value of investing in its personnel in the form of education and training. How often are training opportunities made available for development staff?

❑ Almost all development staff members participate in three or more days of formal continuing education annually.

❑ Some development staff members participate in about two days of formal continuing education annually.

❑ A relatively small number of development staff members participate in minor amounts of formal continuing education most years.

❑ We do not have a budget for continuing education for our development staff members.

Professional Development

Does your organization support the development staff's membership and active participation in the Association of Fundraising Professionals, CharityChannel, or other similar organizations?

❑ All are encouraged to become active members and are given time off to attend meetings and conferences, and their annual dues are paid by our organization.

❑ All may join, but time out of the office is severely limited, and/or dues are only partially reimbursed.

❑ Staff may join and participate at their own expense, and time away from the office is severely limited.

❑ Staff members are discouraged from joining, and/or they may join and participate, all at their own expense (time and money).

Investing in the Development Office

It is important that your organization budget for marketing and the technology to support marketing and development efforts. For example, does it invest in things like computer hardware and software upgrades and updates? Does it employ or engage outside contractors to design professional-looking communications pieces, including your website? Does your organization understand the value of investing in marketing, communications, and appropriate equipment/technology?

❑ Yes, our organization fully understands and is highly committed in this regard.

❑ Yes, our organization pretty much understands and is fairly committed in this regard.

❑ Our organization generally understands and would like to do more, but we lack the resources at this time.

❑ Our organization does not see the need to invest in technology and marketing.

Over-involvement in Non-campaign Tasks

Is your staff free from over-involvement in special events, grant proposal development, marketing, or non-development-related tasks, so that they can focus on the campaign?

❑ We plan to hire additional staff during the campaign.

❑ We have full-time staff people devoted to events, grants, and marketing.

❑ We have part-time staff people devoted to these tasks.

❑ We expect our staff to be able to run the campaign, along with everything else on their plates.

Our staff is overwhelmed with other fundraising activities that will prevent them from devoting sufficient time to the campaign.

❑ Yes.

❑ No.

If your staff does not have sufficient time to devote to the campaign, you may need to hire additional resources or reassign duties among current staff members before launching a campaign.

We will develop a plan to hire additional staff or reassign staff duties. This plan will be completed by the following date _____. The person responsible for this plan(s) is _____. The budget for additional staffing is $_____.

Campaign Experience

If your organization has run a capital campaign in the past, you will want to draw on that experience. Too often, organizations fail to keep campaign donors and volunteers involved in ongoing development efforts. If you've had experience with past campaigns, you can often re-engage volunteers and donors in this and future campaigns.

What has been your organization's experience with a major fundraising campaign?

❑ Within the past three years, we completed a major fundraising campaign.

❑ We completed a major fundraising campaign between three and seven years ago.

❑ Our last major fundraising campaign was seven to twelve years ago.

❑ Our organization has never conducted a major fundraising campaign or has not conducted one for twelve or more years.

How successful was your organization's last major fundraising campaign?

❑ We met or exceeded our announced goal.

❑ We were less than 10 percent short of the goal.

❑ We were more than 10 percent short of the goal.

❑ We have never held a campaign.

Do you have records from past campaigns that include donors, volunteers, staffing, and consultants?

❑ We have a donor database that stores all records from past campaigns, and these records are accurate.

❑ We have records from past campaigns in our database, but we do not believe these records are 100 percent accurate.

❑ We have records from past campaigns in hard copy which we can easily retrieve.

❑ We did not keep good records from our previous campaigns.

Your entire staff is critical to the success of your campaign. All of your staff members should be involved at some level and should be invited to contribute financially and be involved in the management or daily operation of campaign activities.

The development staff, like the CEO, will need to be free from extraneous activities which might take time away from campaign duties. Make sure you have a plan to fully staff your campaign.

After the Campaign

Once your campaign is over and before the glow of success fades, you should think about how your organization can "capitalize" on its success to build a stronger development program and a stronger organization for the future.

One of the major benefits of a successful campaign is that it leaves an organization much stronger than it was before the campaign. The reasons for this are:

◆ The campaign starts with an internal assessment, and that assessment will result in recommendations to strengthen the infrastructure of your organization.

◆ Increased public relations efforts during a campaign result in a heightened awareness of the organization in the community.

◆ Volunteer involvement in the campaign provides future volunteer fundraisers for the organization's ongoing development efforts.

◆ Your staff benefits from working with a consultant and gains knowledge and experience which are assets to them and the organization going forward.

practical tip

If you've previously run a campaign, it will be important to assess past results. Let's develop a plan to do that:

Task	Budget	Person or Team Responsible	Timeline to Complete
Review previous campaign results			
List potential donors from past campaign results			
List potential volunteers from past campaigns			
List what went wrong and what went right in past campaigns			
Develop a plan for this campaign based on previous results			
Develop a post-campaign plan to ensure results of this campaign will be capitalized on			

To Recap

◆ If you've run a campaign previously, search those records for potential donors and volunteers who might be interested in getting involved in this campaign.

◆ All staff members should be involved in the campaign and asked to contribute to it.

◆ Be sure staff members can devote sufficient time to the campaign.

Chapter Eight

Donor Records and Development Office Infrastructure

IN THIS CHAPTER

···→ What type of database do you need to run a campaign?

···→ What policies do you need to have in place before starting a campaign?

···→ What office procedures should be in place to help you manage a campaign?

The Importance of Your Database in the Campaign

Having a single database that will track your campaign information, allow you to communicate with your donors and volunteers, and prepare campaign reports will be critical. If you've never run a campaign before, this might be the first time you've had to track multi-year pledges. If you've never worked with volunteer fundraisers, you might not have needed to track the results of volunteer solicitation calls. If you will need short-term financing, your lender will want to see cash-flow projections for the campaign. Be sure you have a system that can track these things.

How would you describe your organization's giving records?

❏ We have a single, integrated, and always-current donor database managed on a computer with development software. This software was purchased within the past three years or is updated regularly and contains complete donor giving histories for the past five years or more.

❏ We have reliable individual donor giving records for at least the past three to five years on a computer and are using development software; we can usually produce reports and mailings which meet our needs reasonably well.

❑ We have records of almost all individual giving, including most fundraising events, mailings, and/or activities of the past three years, but they are not integrated using development software. Records are in Excel, Access, or some type of database that is not a licensed fundraising software program.

❑ We have almost no permanent records showing gifts received more than about a year ago.

Can you trust that the information on your donor database, including both contact information and donation history, is up-to-date and accurate?

❑ Yes, totally

❑ Yes, for the most part

❑ Not really

❑ Significant gaps or problems exist.

Will your donor database allow you to record and report on campaign pledges and donations, volunteer activity, and other critical donor information?

❑ Yes

❑ No

Fundraising Policies and Procedures

Why is it important to have fundraising policies in place?

Most nonprofit organizations have personnel policies, fiscal policies, and board policies, but often these same organizations have never taken the time to develop fundraising policies. Since you will likely be accepting major donations, gifts in kind, and perhaps unusual gifts, these policies will be especially important during your campaign for a number of reasons:

◆ They prevent you from accepting gifts that may be inappropriate for your organization or the campaign.

◆ They prevent you from accepting gifts that have "strings" attached to them.

◆ Consistent policies prevent your staff from reinventing the wheel if an unusual situation arises during the campaign.

◆ They provide guidelines for volunteers who are making solicitation calls.

◆ They provide guidelines on how to dispose of or invest non-cash gifts.

These are just a few of the dilemmas that some nonprofits have faced:

◆ An environmental agency was faced with a gift from a member of the local business community whose company was a well-known polluter of the environment.

◆ A domestic violence center was offered a major gift from the owner of a "gentlemen's club."

◆ A religious organization was offered a gift of stock from a company that was deemed by this organization to be "socially unacceptable."

◆ An organization located in Nevada was offered a gift from a brothel (a legal business in rural Nevada).

◆ An organization was offered a gift of land, to the delight of its board of directors, who were contemplating a capital campaign for a new facility and needed a building site. The board's excitement turned sour when they found it would cost $500,000 to remediate the soil on this site.

◆ An art museum was offered a "valuable piece of artwork" that turned out to be a painting of Elvis Presley on black velvet, which did not fit into this museum's collection.

◆ A religious organization turned down a major gift from the winner of a lottery because its policy stated that gambling proceeds were not deemed acceptable donations.

◆ A university was offered a large gift with the stipulation that the donor would be appointed to the board of trustees.

This brief sampling of some of the dilemmas that accompany gift acceptance points to the reasons that having these polices, especially when entering a campaign, is important.

stories from the real world

What should these policies cover? Some things to consider when developing gift acceptance policies:

◆ How will gifts be solicited?

◆ From whom will the organization accept gifts?

◆ What types of gifts will be accepted?

◆ How will those gifts be acknowledged and recognized?

◆ How will gifts be disposed of or invested?

◆ What kind of stewardship will be provided to the donor?

Do you have gift acceptance polices in place?

❏ Yes

❏ Yes, but they need work

❏ No

Office procedures are important for all of your development activities, but will be even more critical during a campaign. This might be the first time you've had to deal with multi-year pledges, major donors, and unusual gifts. You need to be prepared for all of these things.

Do you have office procedures in place for accepting, recording, and reporting campaign pledges and donations?

❏ Yes

❏ Yes, but they need work

❏ No

You might need to purchase a new database, upgrade your current system, or train your staff in using the database to track campaign data. In addition, you might need to develop policies and procedures before you start the campaign. This table will help you create a plan to do that now:

Task	Budget	Person or Team Responsible	Timeline to be Completed
Review our current database			
Make decision to purchase new database or upgrade our current system			
Train staff in the use of the database to track campaign information			
Develop gift acceptance policies			
Develop recognition policies			
Develop investment policies			
Develop office procedures			

To Recap

◆ Gift acceptance polices will be important during a campaign because you might be offered gifts of land, property, or other unusual gifts.

◆ Make sure you have procedures in place for receiving, acknowledging, and reporting all campaign gifts and pledges.

◆ An up-to-date donor software system will be critical in managing the campaign.

Chapter Nine

Governance

IN THIS CHAPTER

···→ What role does the board play in a campaign?

···→ Do you need to expand the size of your board for a campaign?

···→ What happens if your board does not support the campaign?

During your feasibility study, you are likely to receive recommendations for strengthening or enlarging your board. The board's role will be critical to the success of your campaign. Without a 100 percent commitment from the board, both in concept and financially, it will be impossible to ask others for support.

Many organizations beef up their boards' involvement in development efforts before starting campaigns. An organization might expand the size of the board, create a development committee, or obtain training and education in fundraising areas for the board. During your feasibility study, you are likely to receive recommendations for strengthening or enlarging your board.

Some basic questions to ask about your board are:

Except for illness or occasional travel, do your organization's board members attend board and committee meetings regularly?

❑ All do

❑ Most do

❑ Some do

❑ A few do

How many of your board members are highly aware of, although perhaps not always in complete agreement with, the organization's mission, programs, history, current challenges, and plans?

❑ All or nearly all

❑ Most or many

❑ Some

❑ Few or none

How many of your board members are comfortably conversant with your organization's mission statement and program?

❑ All

❑ Most

❑ A few

❑ Almost none

❑ No written mission statement

How many of your board members are comfortably conversant with your organization's vision and values statements?

❑ All

❑ Most

❑ A few

❑ Almost none

❑ No written vision and values statements

Just as with other fundraising activities you do on an ongoing basis, board giving will be a critical first step in your campaign. We've probably all heard board giving defined in terms of the three Gs listed above. If board members aren't giving or getting, they should get off the board. This concept might

> **The Traditional Three Gs**
>
> Give,
>
> Get, or
>
> Get Off
>
> **observation**

seem harsh, but it is important to stress the board's financial commitment before you launch a campaign.

Many funders will not contribute until they know the board has made a financial contribution first. Foundations will often ask this question on the application for a grant. Corporations, businesses, and individuals, however, also want to know that the "family" of the organization has supported it with the first commitments before asking others to join them in supporting the campaign.

Another way to look at board giving in a more positive light is to consider my "new three Gs" and think about how you can educate, inspire, and improve your board using these concepts.

The "gather" phase involves assessing your board and its involvement in your development efforts. "Getting ready" means that you develop a plan to identify, recruit, and train board members who are able and willing to give *and* get. With these steps, you will be able to "grow" your board into a powerful force which can help your campaign succeed. Here are some questions to get you started in assessing your board:

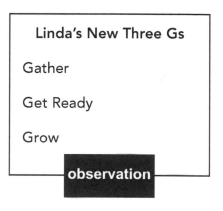

Linda's New Three Gs

Gather

Get Ready

Grow

observation

How many members of your board of directors made a direct financial contribution to your organization last year beyond buying tickets, purchasing goods, etc.?

❑ All

❑ Most

❑ A few

❑ None

Beyond their own giving, how many of your board members help raise funds for your organization?

❑ All

❑ Most

❑ A few

❑ None

How many of your board members are in a position to positively influence others in the community who may impact the success of your organization's campaign (e.g., make major financial contributions and/or provide effective volunteer leadership)?

❑ Most or all

❑ Many

❑ Some

❑ None or almost none

How many of your board members have contacts in the *foundation* world who could help secure grants for your campaign?

❑ Most or all

❑ Many

❑ Some

❑ None or almost none

How many of your board members have contacts in the *business community* who could help secure gifts or grants for your campaign?

❑ Most or all

❑ Many

❑ Some

❑ None or almost none

How many of your board members have contacts with *individual major donors* who could help secure gifts for your campaign?

❑ Most or all

❑ Many

❑ Some

❑ None or almost none

The Role of the Board Chair

The chair of your board will play a particularly important role in the campaign. The board chair is typically the official spokesperson for your organization. Without the chair's support and enthusiasm, it will be difficult to convince people that your organization is ready for a campaign.

Rate the fundraising comfort level of your board president/chair:

❑ Very comfortable; enjoys the process of seeking philanthropic support (including face-to-face asking for the gift) and seeks opportunities to do so

❑ Reasonably comfortable with, and participates in, the process of seeking philanthropic support, including personally asking for the gift face-to-face

❑ Uncomfortable; avoids or delegates directly asking for financial support when possible

❑ Very uncomfortable; will absolutely not ask others face-to-face for financial support

Board/Staff Relations

All organizations have some internal conflict or tension between board and staff. Conflict between the board and the staff can become more apparent during a campaign, when so many volunteers are deeply involved with your organization. Volunteers and donors will quickly sense that relationships within the organization are askew and will be reluctant to support the campaign if the conflict is severe. What is the level of conflict in your organization?

❑ Low

❑ Moderate

❑ High

❑ Very high

Board Education

Building the board's enthusiasm is one of the most critical elements in a capital campaign. But, of course, your board members don't think they need *training*! They don't have time for it, and they won't listen to what you have to say anyway, right?

The first essential step is to avoid the word "training." Use a title, such as *Executive Leadership Institute, Campaign Readiness,* or *Are We Ready for a Capital Campaign?*, for a board "training session." You can do an all-day or half-day training session for the board before launching a campaign, and/or do a series of mini-sessions throughout the campaign. Since you will likely be working with a consultant, that person can help you plan board training that is appropriate for your board.

Leading up to the campaign, you can plan some type of board education at every board meeting—even if it is a five-minute presentation on the *Role of Boards in a Campaign, Ethical Issues in Capital Campaigns*, or *Making the Case for Your Campaign*—you get the idea. For a more intense session, schedule a retreat at a convenient time for most board members, often a Saturday morning or a half-day session in place of, or before, a regular board meeting.

Board education can be done by staff, but is usually more effective when done by an outside resource. A consultant, a board member from another organization, or some other experienced resource can often tell your board the things it needs to hear with a new spin.

As discussed above, you might need to "beef up" your board before starting your capital campaign. Here is a grid to help you plan for your board development:

Task	Budget	Person or Team Responsible	Timeline to Complete
Assess the board's willingness to support this campaign			
Pass board resolution to proceed with campaign			
Ensure 100 percent financial support from the board			
Provide education for the board on the capital campaign and its role in the campaign			
Add new board members if necessary			

To Recap

◆ In your campaign, it is critical to have 100 percent financial participation by your board before asking others to contribute.

◆ If there is conflict among the board and the staff, resolve it before launching your campaign.

◆ Educate your board on capital campaigns and the board's role in the campaign early in the process.

Chapter Ten

Volunteer Roles and Responsibilities

IN THIS CHAPTER

····→ How many volunteers do you need to run a campaign?

····→ What are the roles of campaign volunteers?

····→ Where can you find volunteers?

In my opinion, volunteer campaign leadership is the single most important factor in campaign success. The right campaign chair can inspire volunteers, donors, board members, and staff. Volunteers bring to the table contacts, cash, and clout. Choose your volunteer leadership wisely because volunteers can make or break your campaign.

Campaign Leadership

It will be vital to recruit a potential campaign chair or co-chairs with all of the following qualities:

◆ Passion for your need or organization

◆ Willingness to make a leadership gift or one that will stretch the individual's normal giving pattern

◆ Positive influence with people of wealth

◆ Time to devote to the campaign

◆ Leadership skills

Sometimes campaign leadership is recruited too early because organizations want to get moving with the campaign. Caution: think through who would make the best chair for your campaign. Review the list of qualities above and then determine whether:

❑ We have identified one or more people who have all of these qualities, and those who have been identified have agreed to serve in this capacity.

❑ We have identified one or more people who have most or all of these qualities, but have not yet asked these people to serve in this capacity.

❑ We have not yet identified anyone with either most or all of these qualities.

❑ We have already asked someone who possesses some, but not all, of these qualities to serve as our campaign chair.

Recruiting and Working with Capital Campaign Volunteers

Capital campaign volunteers are a critical component of a successful campaign. So where do you find these volunteers, and how do you manage the process? The names acquired during the planning study are a good place to start. You can begin by recruiting campaign cabinet members who displayed an interest in the project or were suggested by interviewers. Then add to the list of potential volunteers through strategy meetings with the board, staff, and consultants.

Remember that the campaign chair, co-chairs, or office of the chair is *the most* critical role in the campaign. This person or these persons must be selected carefully and should be able to inspire, motivate, and lead the rest of the campaign cabinet to success. Here are some steps to follow in recruiting volunteer leadership for your campaign:

◆ Always have a job description for every volunteer.

◆ Develop the job description *first,* and then find the right person to fill each role.

◆ Once the job descriptions are in place and a list of potential volunteers to fill each position is in place, develop a volunteer recruitment packet with the job description, the campaign timeline, the campaign organizational chart, the case for support, and other pertinent information about the organization and the campaign.

◆ Select the campaign cabinet members and provide them with suggestions for volunteers for their committees based on suggestions received in the planning study, from the strategy sessions, and from other cabinet members.

◆ Hold regularly scheduled campaign cabinet meetings at times and locations that are convenient for the majority of the cabinet members. Meetings are usually monthly unless your campaign will run three years or more, in which case you might opt for bi-monthly or quarterly cabinet meetings.

◆ Insist on training and ongoing report meetings for volunteers who will solicit donors during the period in which these volunteers will be actively soliciting for the campaign.

◆ Provide a fundraising mentor for committee members who are newer at fundraising.

◆ Stay in close contact with volunteers through e-mails and phone calls to update them on campaign news, inquire on the status of their calls, and inform them of anything that causes a change in the campaign plan.

◆ Set up a special website page just for campaign volunteers so they can stay on top of campaign development conveniently and throughout the campaign.

It will usually take hundreds of volunteers to run a capital campaign, unless your campaign is small or narrowly focused. You will need a job description for each of these volunteers, and you will need to provide campaign training for them. Here is a tool to help you plan for volunteer recruitment:

Task	Budget	Person or Team Responsible	Timeline to Complete
Determine the number of people needed on the campaign cabinet			
Develop position descriptions for these volunteers			
Recruit campaign cabinet			
Determine how many other volunteers are needed			
Develop position descriptions for volunteers			
Recruit volunteers			
Provide campaign training for all volunteers			

To Recap

◆ Campaign volunteers can make or break your campaign, so choose volunteers wisely.

◆ Determine all of the campaign phases that volunteers will be involved in.

◆ Before talking to prospective volunteers, be sure to have a campaign plan that includes a job description for each volunteer position.

Chapter Eleven

Developing a Plan for a Successful Campaign

IN THIS CHAPTER

···→ How do you get started with a campaign?

···→ How long will it take us to run a campaign, and how much will it cost?

···→ What happens if you're not ready for a campaign?

If you've read this book and filled out all of the answers to the questions posed, and you feel that you're in pretty good shape to begin your campaign, what's next?

First of all, you want to get the approval to launch a campaign from your board of directors. You need to think about the timeline for your campaign, the budget, and how the campaign will fit into your overall development program.

Campaign Budget

How large a budget for campaign expenses have you included as part of your total campaign goal?

❑ 10 percent to 15 percent of the goal

❑ 5 percent to 10 percent of the goal

❑ Less than 5 percent of the goal

❑ No amount included

Campaign costs typically run anywhere from 8 percent to 12 percent of your overall goal. Many factors affect the costs of your campaign. For example:

◆ Whether you're using campaign counsel, how much support you need from counsel, and whether the counsel is local, regional, or national

◆ Whether you need to hire additional staff to support the campaign management

◆ Whether your campaign is national or international in scope and how much travel it will require

◆ How long the campaign will run

Almost every organization that plans a capital campaign engages a consultant to help. While hiring a consultant isn't an absolute guarantee of success, it can help overcome some campaign roadblocks. For example, a consultant can:

◆ Ensure that staff members stay focused on campaign activities

◆ Develop a plan for recruiting and educating campaign volunteers

◆ Provide the expertise to plan and execute a campaign

The cost of hiring a consultant will depend on the size and location of the firm, the degree of experience of the consultant assigned to your campaign, and the amount of time the consultant will need to spend on your campaign.

Go back and review Chapters Five and Six, focusing on the role of consultants and determine what services you need before completing your budget.

Timeline

Most campaigns will take at least eighteen months to two years to complete, but again, the answer to how long your campaign will run is … it depends.

It depends on the financial goal of your campaign, how many leadership gift prospects you have, and the geographic scope of your campaign. Other factors that impact the timeline include recruitment of volunteer leadership and staff availability. And don't forget—you need to add time for planning, time to conduct a study, and possible delays in getting permits, purchasing land, and securing architectural plans.

Use the table below to develop a timeline for your pre-campaign planning:

Task	Budget	Person or Team Responsible	Timeline to Complete
Determine size and scope of project			
Purchase land if needed			
Complete architectural plans			
Establish a preliminary goal for the campaign			
Conduct a planning study			

If you are ready for a campaign, this grid should help you get all your ducks in a row:

Task	Budget	Person or Team Responsible	Timeline to Complete
Engage campaign counsel			
Create an overall development plan that incorporates the campaign into long-range planning			
Develop a campaign budget			
Recruit campaign volunteers			
Develop the campaign case statement			
Secure 100 percent commitment from your board			
Conduct staff appeal			
Develop prospect lists			
Recruit campaign leadership			
Recruit campaign cabinet			
Conduct quiet phase of campaign			
Hold campaign kickoff event			
Conduct public phase of campaign			
Wrap up campaign and plan dedication event			

What If We're Not Ready?

If, after going through this workbook, you've determined that your organization is not ready for a campaign at this time, is all lost?

No!

My hope is that, for those of you who find yourselves ready, this book will provide you with the guidance you need to run a successful campaign. Furthermore, if you find that you are *not* ready, I hope this book will provide you with the tools to help strengthen your organization for a future campaign.

But what if you need the space, the equipment, or the renovations *now*? What if you *can't* wait? There are some other options you can consider:

◆ Running a campaign in phases, addressing the most critical needs first

◆ Financing your project through a line of credit or other short-term financing

◆ Delaying the expansion of your program until you can build the required facilities or provide the equipment needed for these services

◆ Collaborating with another nonprofit to provide the services you would provide in an expanded space

A phased campaign is often the answer. The advantages of this approach are twofold: you can bite off a manageable chunk of the campaign, and often, a successful small campaign will help you prepare for a more comprehensive campaign later. The disadvantage is that you can end up in a perpetual campaign mode, which sometimes leads to staff, volunteer, and donor fatigue. However, if you time your campaign right and make it clear from the beginning that you are running a phased campaign, this approach can be ideal.

Obtaining a loan to build or renovate is often a good approach, as well. Don't go into this plan with the idea that later, when you are ready, you will run a debt-reduction campaign. It's hard to raise money for debt reduction; most debt reduction campaigns are not successful because donors think you didn't plan well if you expanded programs and services when you couldn't afford to do so. Sometimes debt reduction can be included in a larger campaign as part of the project. For example, you might try to raise $1,000,000 to pay off debt while raising $8,000,000 for a new expansion.

As hard as it is to delay expansion of your programs because you simply are not ready for a campaign, sometimes this is the only answer. Engage your organization in a strategic planning process to determine whether the programs are actually needed and then, if they are, see if there is some other channel of delivery. If the programs are truly time-critical, you might need to lease space or collaborate with another organization to provide immediate program delivery before you can house them yourself.

If you are not ready for a campaign, go back to Chapters Two, Six, Eight, Nine, and Ten and review what you've learned about the importance of board commitment, staffing infrastructure, public awareness, donor prospects, and volunteer involvement. These are usually the areas where most organizations find their weaknesses. See what you can do in these areas to strengthen your organization.

Even if you decide not to launch a campaign, strengthening your organization in these areas will help you become stronger in the long run and may help increase your annual giving, as well. Who knows? You might even find that you can raise enough money in your annual giving program to fund some of the capital expenses you need to expand your program.

Whatever you determine is best for your organization, I hope this book has helped you prepare for success.

To Recap

◆ If you find you are indeed ready for a campaign, start your pre-campaign planning now. Good planning takes time.

◆ If you determine that you are not ready for a campaign, begin to prepare your staff, board, and volunteers for the time you are ready to launch your campaign.

◆ Go back to the strategic planning process and determine what your options are for maintaining or expanding programs and activities while you are preparing for your campaign.

Appendix A

Donor Bill of Rights

A Donor Bill of Rights
Philanthropy is based on voluntary action for the common good. It is a tradition of giving and sharing that is primary to the quality of life. To assure that philanthropy merits the respect and trust of the general public, and that donors and prospective donors can have full confidence in the not-for-profit organizations and causes they are asked to support, we declare that all donors have these rights:

I. To be informed of the organization's mission, of the way the organization intends to use donated resources, and of its capacity to use donations effectively for their intended purposes.	**VI.** To be assured that information about their donations is handled with respect and with confidentiality to the extent provided by law.
II. To be informed of the identity of those serving on the organization's governing board, and to expect the board to exercise prudent judgment in its stewardship responsibilities.	**VII.** To expect that all relationships with individuals representing organizations of interest to the donor will be professional in nature.
III. To have access to the organization's most recent financial statements.	**VIII.** To be informed whether those seeking donations are volunteers, employees of the organization or hired solicitors.
IV. To be assured their gifts will be used for the purposes for which they were given.	**IX.** To have the opportunity for their names to be deleted from mailing lists that an organization may intend to share.
V. To receive appropriate acknowledgment and recognition.	**X.** To feel free to ask questions when making a donation and to receive prompt, truthful and forthright answers.
Developed by: (AAFRC) American Association of Fund Raising Counsel (AHP) Association for Healthcare Philanthropy (CASE) Council for Advancement & Support of Education (AFP) Association of Fundraising Professionals	Endorsed by: Independent Sector National Catholic Development Conference (NCDC) Partnership for Philanthropic Planning (PPP) National Council for Resource Development (NCRD) United Way of America

Index

If you enjoyed this book, you'll want to pick up the other books in the CharityChannel Press **In the Trenches™** series.

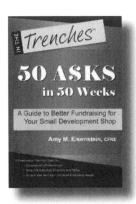

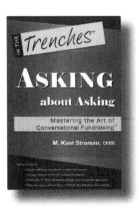

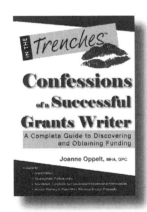

And dozens more coming soon!

www.CharityChannel.com

And now introducing **For the GENIUS® Press,** an imprint that produces books on just about any topic that people want to learn. You don't have to be a genius to read a **GENIUS** book, but you'll sure be smarter once you do!

Fundraising for the GENIUS™

The only book you'll ever need to raise more money for your nonprofit organization.

FOR THE GENIUS IN ALL OF US™

Linda Lysakowski, ACFRE

www.ForTheGENIUS.com

for the GENIUS
PRESS

Made in the USA
Lexington, KY
10 May 2013